THE
SPECIAL EDUCATION
HANDBOOK

A Comprehensive Guide for Parents and Educators

THE
SPECIAL EDUCATION
HANDBOOK
A Comprehensive Guide for
Parents and Educators

KENNETH SHORE

Foreword by Betty B. Osman

TEACHERS
COLLEGE
PRESS

Teachers College, Columbia University
New York and London

Published by Teachers College Press, 1234 Amsterdam Avenue, New York, N.Y. 10027

Library of Congress Cataloging in Publication Data

Shore, Kenneth.

The special education handbook.

Bibliography: p.
Includes index.
1. Handicapped children—Education—United States.
2. Individualized Instruction. I. Title.
LC 4031.S46   1986   371.9   86-1801

ISBN 0-8077-2806-3 (pbk.)

Manufactured in the United States of America

91 90 89 88 87   2 3 4 5 6

To Maxine

Contents

Foreword

For the first time in our history, parents of handicapped children have been given the responsibility as well as the right to participate in their children's education. It was actually through the efforts of parents who were frustrated in their attempts to gain an appropriate education for their handicapped children that Public law 94–142 was passed. The law, which became effective in September, 1978, mandates the inclusion of parents in the decision-making process when there is a need for special education services.

Yet almost ten years later, a majority of parents neither assume the right granted by Federal law nor accept the responsibility they fought so hard to gain. There are varied reasons for this lack of parental participation. A number of working parents may find such involvement too time-consuming or difficult to arrange. Other parents may feel they do not know enough about the process to contribute to the discussions or the decisions about their child's education. Still others may be reluctant to have their children identified as 'handicapped.'

The vast majority of parents, however, are simply unaware of their rights and those of their children, confused by the Individualized Education Programs (IEP's), and intimidated by those in authority at school. Unfortunately, ignorance of the law and its provisions threatens to undermine the significant progress made on behalf of children already involved in the special education process and may imperil the rights of parents and children in the future.

This comprehensive book, primarily addressed to parents, will provide them with an understanding of the legislation and the procedures through which they can best serve as advocates for their children. In clear, straightforward language, Kenneth Shore explains the special education process from the initial referral through the diagnostic evaluation, to the implementation of recommended programs and services. In addition, he details the major provisions of Federal legislation and clarifies parents' rights with respect to school records, proceedings involved in identification, educational practices and programs, and legal safeguards.

This book demystifies special education by explaining the relevant laws, practices, and terminology; suggesting specific questions parents might ask; and discussing specific ways that their views can be incorporated into the educational program. Anticipating parents' fears and concerns, Dr. Shore has included a list of warning signs that might suggest the presence of an educational disability. He describes the tests most frequently used in the evaluation process and clarifies commonly held misconceptions to allay parents' anxieties. He carefully guides parents through the steps necessary to secure for their children the programs and support they need. An entire chapter of the book focuses on preparing parents to be effective participants in the special education process. It pinpoints potential obstacles and offers communication strategies that may be helpful in dealing with children, teachers, administrators, and policy makers.

This is an important book, filled with useful information for parents of children with a variety of handicapping conditions. We cannot afford to take special education for granted, nor lose the momentum gained in the last decade. Parents who adopt the strategies outlined in this book will be well-prepared to participate in the special education process and ensure their children the appropriate education and resources to which they are legally entitled.

Betty B. Osman, Ph.D.
Scarsdale, New York

Introduction

A parent is worth 10,000 schoolmasters.
—Chinese proverb

Parents of children with special needs have reason to remember November 29, 1975. On that day, President Gerald Ford signed into law the *Education for All Handicapped Children Act* (Public Law 94–142). Hailed as an educational bill of rights for children with educational disabilities, this federal law not only required that "all handicapped children have available to them a free appropriate public education" but also dramatically expanded parents' roles in their children's education.

The framers of Public Law 94–142 hoped to forge an alliance between parents and schools on behalf of children with special needs. In practice, however, this has not always been a partnership of equals. Many parents have been reluctant or unable to take part in the design and support of their children's special education programs. Some are intimidated by school staff or by educators' jargon; others fear that they have little to offer; still others don't understand the special education maze or lack the communication skills or the confidence to express their views and wishes.

This book attempts to redress that balance by providing you—the parent—with information and skills that can help you to participate as full and active partners in the special education of your child. It provides a comprehensive understanding of the special education process—including identification and referral, evaluation, educational placement and programming, and conflict resolution; it details procedures that school districts must follow; it spells out your rights and your children's rights; and it describes communication skills that can help you negotiate your way through the labyrinth of special education. The focus is on providing practical information to strengthen your grasp of special education practices and to ensure that the educational program planned for your child takes your ideas and views into account. While it addresses parents, this book can also be used by professionals who work either in or out of the school setting with children who have special needs.

Why is your role as parent so crucial? Quite simply, you offer a combination of knowledge, influence, concern, and commitment that is unique. You are your child's first and best teacher. You have instructed your child since birth and have observed him or her in a variety of settings, in a range of situations, in myriad activities. In the process, you have developed a profound understanding of your child. Because of your expertise, your perspective is vital to the process that leads to sound educational decisions.

You provide more than information. You offer a commitment to your child more tenacious than that of any other person. With this commitment comes a desire to secure the best education for your child, and often the determination to ensure that your hopes are realized. For this reason, your involvement in the special education process is the surest way of protecting the educational interests of your child, and the best method of ensuring the school district's accountability. Research supports this view: studies have shown that parents' involvement in their children's special education programs enhances academic performance and improves classroom behavior.

In short, no one knows as much about your child as you do, no one cares as much for your child as you do, and no one will fight as hard for your child's rights as you will. My aim is not to give you information about your child—for you are the real authority on that subject—but rather to help you mobilize your expertise and commitment so that you can be an effective advocate for your son or daughter as you work with the school to meet your child's educational needs.

As you read this book, keep the following points in mind:

• This book addresses parents of children who have a range of educational disabilities. Some sections may speak directly to your own particular needs; some may not. But if you have an interest in special education, you will find most of this book relevant, no matter what your child's special needs may be.

• This book describes a range of actions that you might take on behalf of your child. Of course, you need not follow each and every suggestion. Decide for yourself how involved you wish to be in your child's special education program based on your own situation. Some parents may choose to participate intensively; others may become less involved.

• This book describes the special education process as it is supposed to work. Recognizing that the process has sometimes fallen short of the ideals embodied in Public Law 94–142, I have also highlighted potential trouble spots—points at which the process is prone to breaking down—and have suggested possible remedies or responses.

• Because of space limitation, some topics receive only cursory treatment. Readers who wish to pursue issues in greater depth will find additional sources of information listed at each chapter's end.

• The appendix contains information of practical value, including a list of warning signs that may alert you to an area where your child might have a possible educational disability; a listing of organizations and information resources; and a glossary to help you make sense of special education terminology.

• School districts in all fifty states must conform to the federal laws described in this book. You may also want to consult your own state's special education code for additional regulations. You also need to be alert to changes in federal and state regulations that may affect your child's education.

I want to acknowledge a number of people who made important contributions to this book. I am indebted to the many parents of children with special needs with whom I have worked and from whom I have received a special education. My thanks also to the following persons who lent their expertise in reviewing portions of this book and who provided many valuable suggestions: Marilyn Arons, Joanne Bergen, Buzz Bronicki, Joan Henry, Kenneth Koehly, Carol Lidz, Wayne I. Newland, and Barbara Semkow. I am especially grateful to Rima Shore for her editorial expertise; her keen eye and creative hand and her gift of clarity made the book more fluent and readable. Finally, I owe a special debt of gratitude to my wife Maxine for her generous contributions of time, patience, and encouragement. Without her, this book would not have been possible.

1

Special Education:
An Overview

Darrell is puzzled by his reading problem. He can't understand why reading seems a cinch for many of his classmates, and such a struggle for him. He entered the fourth grade this year reading at a mid-second grade level and is still finding it hard to "break the code." Yet his comprehension is good: when a story is read to him, his understanding matches that of the other children in his class. Darrell is not a good speller, but except for word problems math comes easily to him, and he is in the top math group in his class. Darrell's learning problem has not affected his good peer relationships nor dampened his enthusiasm for board games. He is class champion at *Trivial Pursuit*. A few months ago he started getting specialized help in reading for an hour each day in a setting called a resource room. He still trails his classmates in reading, but he is able to grasp the material his special education teacher provides, and visible signs of progress have buoyed his spirits.

Maria is a fourteen-year-old who has been blind since birth due to retrolental fibroplasia, a condition caused by excessive oxygen in the incubator she occupied in the first days of life. Her other senses are unimpaired. She knows her teachers by their footsteps and she seems to remember everything she hears. With the exception of braille instruction three periods a week and a specialized gym program, Maria has followed the same academic program as her sighted peers. Using such aids as braille and recorded books, a braille writer and a typewriter, Maria has generally received grades of B and C. She has a lively sense of humor and is well liked in school, although she rarely gets together with her classmates outside of school. Maria enjoys reading (she can read braille at the rate of ninety-five words per minute), but her best subject is math. She is excited about the prospect of using computers with braille adaptation.

A thirteen-year-old seventh grader, Donald has challenged almost every teacher he has had to spark the academic potential that standardized test scores indicated was above average, and to control his angry outbursts and disruptive behavior. Some teachers have been more successful than others, but even with those to whom he responded best, Donald was unpredictable—cooperative one day, defiant the next. When he entered middle school last year, his problems escalated. If there was a fight, chances are Donald was involved. When he showed up in class—which, between cuts and suspensions, was only two-thirds of the time—he would slouch in the back row and either doze off or disrupt class with inappropriate comments or noises. This year, the school completed a comprehensive evaluation of his psychological and educational status and revised Donald's program. He now spends three periods a day in a special education class with seven other students where he receives instruction in English, math, and science, and where the teacher can address his behavior problems and his underlying emotional needs. He spends the other four periods in regular education classes where his behavior has been only occasionally troublesome.

Ruth is a seventeen-year-old high school junior whose intellectual and academic development have been much slower than that of her peers. She is mentally retarded. She has always had difficulty keeping up with other children in school although she could sometimes hold her own when she could take advantage of her reliable memory. Before long, as the schoolwork hinged less on memory and more on understanding, her problems became more apparent and her frustration mounted. Not until she entered a special education class in third grade for her academic subjects did she realize that there were other children who had similar difficulties. As Ruth began to find areas in which she could succeed (for example, she took part in the hundred-yard dash at the Special Olympics two years in a row), she became more confident and assertive. She has taken an active interest in horseback riding, to which she was introduced in summer camp. Ruth is planning a career in the food-service industry, which she is studying in a specialized vocational program.

SPECIAL EDUCATION TODAY

These students have very different educational profiles but share a common learning experience: they all attend public school. And they all have educational disabilities: a specific problem is interfering with their ability to learn effectively in an instructional setting that relies solely on regular education methods. Each receives a program that is specially designed to meet his or her unique educational needs and allows contact with students who are not disabled.

That students with disabilities should attend a public school where they have regular contact with the school's general population is an idea of recent vintage. Indeed, the youngsters described above would likely have been treated very differently if they had walked into a public school building, say, fifteen or twenty years ago. Darrell, the reading-disabled youngster, might have been placed in a special education class with students of all different handicaps and with virtually no contact with other fourth graders. Or, he might have received no services at all. Maria might have been transferred to a special school for the blind, and her prospects for the future might have been narrow. After repeated attempts to discipline Donald, school authorities might have limited his schooling to home instruction. And Ruth, the retarded adolescent, might have been excluded altogether from public education rather than placed in the full-day special education program she now attends.

Strategies for educating the students with special needs have undergone far-reaching change. To appreciate these dramatic strides, we need not journey too far back into history. While local programs for educating children with disabilities were initiated in the early part of this century, these programs were markedly different from the special education programs of the 1980s. They were typically limited to students with mild disabilities, and the school day and school year were usually shorter than for other students. Moreover, classrooms were often small and inadequate and students with special needs were typically segregated from the school's general population.

The watershed occurred during the 1970s when parents and advocacy groups turned to the courts to establish specific educational rights for students with disabilities. Two federal cases were particularly instrumental in establishing the legal right of these children to an appropriate education. The first, *Pennsylvania Association for Retarded Citizens (PARC)* v. *Commonwealth of Pennsylvania* (1971), affirmed the principle that mentally retarded children have the right to a public education. The second, *Mills* v. *Board of Education* (1972), extended the right of public education to all children with handicapping conditions, regardless of the nature or severity of the disability, and established the important principles that: (1) public schools must provide students who have disabilities with alternative educational programs rather than exclude them from school; and (2) school districts cannot refuse to provide educational programs for these students because of a lack of resources.

Despite these advances, the educational rights of people with disabilities were comprehensive neither in scope nor geography. There were fifty different American special education systems: some states offered extensive services while others provided meager services that met legal requirements but dealt with a very narrow range of disabling conditions.

It became increasingly clear that only federal action would resolve the wide discrepancy in the quality of special education services nationwide. Congress responded with two landmark legislative acts: Section 504 of the *Rehabilitation Act of 1973* and Public Law 94–142, the *Education for All Handicapped Children Act of 1975.*

FEDERAL SPECIAL EDUCATION LEGISLATION

Education has, in the United States, always been presumed to be a state and local responsibility. Local control of the schools has been a long cherished tradition. At the same time, the Constitution obligates the federal government to guarantee to all citizens equal rights under the law. In this sense, federal legislation regarding the education of youngsters with special needs is less an attempt to preempt state and local obligations than to ensure that children who have disabilities receive educational services comparable to those extended to children who do not.

Before turning to the provisions of Section 504 and Public Law 94–142, we might give some thought to a few basic concepts of special education legislation. As a rule, states must adhere to the requirements of federal law. They may, of course, do more than federal law requires (as many states have done in developing their own special education codes), but they cannot do less. In other words, state law can be more stringent than federal law, but never more permissive. Understanding the special education process and requirements in a particular state therefore requires familiarity with born federal and state law.

Educational legislation, whether state or federal, is accompanied by regulations that spell out, often in elaborate detail, how the legislation is to be carried out. These regulations, which have the force of law, are usually written by executive agencies—typically the U.S. Office of Education at the federal level, and the state department of education. These agencies may also prepare interpretations of the laws or regulations to clarify their meaning.

Section 504

By passing the civil rights bill known as Section 504 of the Rehabilitation Act of 1973, Congress expressed a national commitment to eliminate discrimination against the disabled. The law resembles, almost word for word, federal laws prohibiting racial and sexual discrimination. The bill stipulates that children who have disabilities must receive educational services and opportunities equal to those provided to children who do not. For example, a school district that provides a 180-day school year for most students, but a 140-day school year for students with disabilities would likely be found in violation of Section 504. A school district that provides a preschool program or computer-assisted instruction for its general population would be obligated to provide comparable programs for children who have disabilities. Section 504 would also prohibit a school district from excluding students with disabilities from a school that is otherwise appropriate, or from appropriate programs within that school, because the building is not physically accessible to them.

Public Law 94—142

Public Law 94–142 (the 142d bill passed into public law by the 94th Congress) seeks "to assure that all handicapped children have available to them . . . a free appropriate public education." The most comprehensive piece of legislation ever passed by Congress involving the education of students with special needs, it has been hailed by many as an "educational bill of rights" for people who have disabilities. Its significance is enhanced by the fact that unlike most legislative acts, Public Law 94–142 is permanent legislation that does not need to be renewed periodically. Unless it is repealed, it is the law of the land forever.

Major Provisions of Federal Legislation

Together, the two federal laws represent a comprehensive legislative mandate to provide free appropriate educational programs to "all handicapped children." While Public Law 94–142 is specific to people age three to twenty-one, and Section 504 applies to persons of any age, the two laws provide many of the same safeguards. In relation to education, they protect the rights of students who have disabilities and the rights of their parents, and impose many of the same obligations upon school districts in educating these students. The essential components of these laws, as they relate to the education of students with special needs, are summarized below and will be discussed in detail in subsequent chapters.

Educational Opportunity. This fundamental principle of federal special education law requires that *all* children who have handicapping conditions, regardless of the nature or severity of the disability, have the opportunity to receive a free appropriate education and are not excluded from public school because of their disability. Public Law 94–142 mandates that states make available a free appropriate public education to *all* "handicapped children" from ages five to eighteen, and also to children age three to five or eighteen to twenty-one unless state law or a court order says otherwise. (Some states have chosen to provide free educational services to children under the age of three who have special needs.) To realize this goal, state departments of education and local school districts must establish procedures to identify and evaluate all children who have disabilities, from birth to age twenty-one, in such settings as public and private schools, residential facilities, and correctional institutions. The school district's level of federal funding depends on the number of its students who receive special education.

Nondiscriminatory Evaluation. Federal law requires that all students who appear to be educationally disabled receive a comprehensive evaluation that fairly assesses their abilities and does not discriminate against them because of cultural or racial factors or a disabling condition. This provision seeks to ensure that the designation of a disabling condition is accurate and that the educational decisions that follow from it are appropriate.

Individualized Education Program. Public Law 94–142 requires that an Individualized Education Program (commonly abbreviated as IEP) be developed for all students who have disabilities and who receive special education services. The backbone of the special education process, the IEP is the formal mechanism by which the goal of an appropriate education is to be realized. By law, it must be designed by a team composed of educators, the student's parent(s), and the student (if appropriate), and must contain specific components. It must describe an educational program based on the child's educational needs, not on the district's resources. Finally, the IEP must be implemented as written.

Least Restrictive Environment. No provision of federal special education law has sparked more controversy or created more confusion than that of the "least restrictive environment." In brief, this principle requires that students who have special needs be educated in a setting which, while meeting their educational requirements, most closely matches the regular education program offered to their schoolmates. Put another way, students who have disabilities must be offered as much of the regular education program as is compatible with their learning and behavioral characteristics. This requirement rests on the premise that special education students profit from contact with their peers in the school's general population. It has often been misread as a mandate for the transfer of special education students to regular education (or "mainstream") settings regardless of their needs. Congress never intended such an interpretation. (In fact, Public Law 94–142 never uses the word "mainstreaming.") Rather, the "least restrictive environment" is to be determined in the context of each student's educational needs: for one student, it may be a regular class for most of the day with special education assistance in a resource room; for another, it may be a special education class for all academic subjects; for still another, a special school.

Due Process. The principle of due process, embodied in the Constitution's Fourteenth Amendment, requires that all persons shall be treated fairly by a governing body and be afforded an opportunity to contest a governmental decision about themselves. Applied to special education, due process requires that educational decisions be reached fairly with genuine regard for the views and wishes of you, the parent, and that decisions be open to your challenge. Both Public Law 94–142 and Section 504 delineate a range of due-process procedures to protect your rights and the rights of your child and provide you with opportunities for challenging school decisions. School districts must comply with these legal safeguards, which are described below.

- *Surrogate Parents.* If a child's parents cannot be identified or located or if the child is a ward of the state, the school district must assign a surrogate parent (called an "educational advocate" in some states)—a knowledgeable individual who acts in the parent's place and represents the child's educational interests.

• *Notice.* Public Law 94–142 requires the school district to inform parents in writing before it initiates or changes, or refuses to initiate or change "the identification, evaluation, or educational placement of the child or the provision of a free appropriate public education to the child." This notice must be in a format clearly understandable to you, the parent, must describe the action proposed or refused and the other options considered, must explain the basis for the action, and must explain the procedural safeguards available to you.

• *Consent.* Written parental consent is required before a school district can conduct a preplacement evaluation or place your youngster in a special education program for the first time.

• *Independent Evaluation.* As parents of a child who has been evaluated by a school district, you are entitled to an additional evaluation by a team of professionals who are not affiliated with the school district. This evaluation is without cost to you if a school district agrees to pay for it or if a hearing officer determines that the school's evaluation is inappropriate.

• *Access to Education Records.* You as parent are entitled to examine all school records relating to your child. The school district is obligated to protect the confidentiality of these records and as a general rule cannot release information to persons or organizations outside the district without your written consent. Chapter 2 has more to say about school records.

• *Impartial Due-Process Hearing.* You may initiate a due-process hearing to challenge a school district's decision regarding the identification, evaluation, or educational placement of your child or your child's right to a free appropriate public education. The school district is also entitled to initiate a hearing on any of these matters.

SUMMARY OF DUE-PROCESS RIGHTS

You must be informed in writing before a school or school district initiates or changes a special education evaluation or program;

refuses to initiate or change a special education evaluation or
   program.

You must give your written consent before a school or school district
      can
   conduct a preplacement evaluation;
   place your child in a special education program for the first time;
   release your child's records to persons or organizations outside
      the school district (with a few exceptions).

You have the right to
   initiate an additional evaluation by professionals outside the school
      district;
   examine all school records pertaining to your child;
   initiate a due-process hearing to challenge a school district's de-
      cision regarding special education for your child.

The existence of a law is reassuring, setting a legal standard to
which most school districts conform. Respect for the law, professional ethics, and concern for the best interests of its students are most
often sufficient to motivate compliance; if not, the desire to hold onto
federal and state funding is reason enough to comply with the law. But
the existence of a law is no guarantee that it will be followed. If you
believe the school district has not lived up to its obligations to evaluate and place your child appropriately, and has not involved you in the
decision-making process, make use of the due-process rights outlined
in this chapter. Chapter 7 discusses procedures you can follow if you
disagree with the school's recommendations or actions.

The Parent's Role in the Special Education Process.   In a partici-
patory democracy, people have the right to take part in making decisions that affect them. The law extends this principle to the special
education process: you as a parent, and, when appropriate, your child,
have the right to share in making educational decisions. This is not only
a matter of fairness; it is sound educational practice. You probably hold
no degrees in education, but you are an expert on your daughter or
son. You can contribute this expertise to an assessment of your child
and to the development of an appropriate educational program. Indeed, research suggests that parents' participation in the special education process helps to bolster their child's academic performance and
social adjustment.
   Federal law, particularly Public Law 94–142, provides opportun-

ities for parental involvement at virtually every step of the special education process. (*Parent* is defined in that law as "a parent, a guardian, a person acting as a parent of a child, or a surrogate parent" so that, for example, a grandmother or step-parent who raises a child has a parent's rights.) Chapter 5, which focuses on the role of parents in the special education process, pinpoints areas where you might become involved.

WHAT'S SPECIAL ABOUT SPECIAL EDUCATION?

Public Law 94-142 defines special education as follows:

> Specially designed instruction, at no cost to parents or guardians, to meet the unique needs of a handicapped child, including classroom instruction, instruction in physical education, home instruction, and instruction in hospitals and institutions.

We can fill out this legal description by listing several distinguishing features of special education:

- comprehensive evaluation of the student's learning and behavioral characteristics;
- intensive instruction precisely matched to the student's educational needs;
- use of specialized materials and equipment, if necessary;
- teachers trained in the education of the students who have special needs;
- ongoing monitoring of student's progress as well as the appropriateness of the program and revision, if necessary.

Special education today is founded on the conviction that if these principles are conscientiously applied, all children who have disabilities will be able to learn, regardless of the nature or severity of their disability. While special education encompasses all of these characteristics, its most salient feature is the careful matching of instruction with a student's unique educational needs and learning style. Education that falls short of this criterion may take place in a special education setting, but it is *not* special education. Special education is an approach, not a place.

Special education can take place in a range of instructional settings, including the regular classroom. It may be provided by specialists or nonspecialists. Indeed, with the "least restrictive environment" mandate of Public Law 94–142, more and more special education students receive instruction in regular education settings from regular classroom teachers. Such an arrangement, however, requires that the teacher have adequate time, resources, and support from educational specialists to gear instruction to the student's individual needs.

Just as special education is not limited to a particular setting, it is not limited to a particular academic focus. As a special education student, your child may receive instruction in any area which, in your view and that of a team of professionals, contributes significantly to his or her education, including "related-service" areas such as speech and language therapy, occupational therapy, or adaptive physical education.

As part of the Individualized Education Program (IEP) team, you share responsibility for designing your child's program. It is critical that the team not base program decisions on overly narrow expectations of your child's academic potential; it should not automatically exclude instruction in any area or subject because of the disability. Many special education students can handle challenging academic material and grasp high-level concepts if the instruction is presented in a way that suits their style of learning.

WHO QUALIFIES?

Special education students comprise a diverse group with a broad spectrum of learning and behavioral characteristics: Sarah stammers, but she is emotionally well adjusted. Harry, a high school junior who has cerebral palsy, is a gifted creative writer. William has emotional and behavior problems, and has reached the seventh grade without learning to read. Eileen has a severe neurological disability and at age nineteen is learning to dress herself. Jenny, a fifth-grader, has a mild hearing impairment. Reuben is a bright preschooler who shows signs of problems with gross-motor movement. All are candidates for special education. The common denominator is that they have educational needs significantly different from those of most regular education students of their age, to the extent that specialized instruction is necessary to help them learn commensurate with their abilities. Put another way, special education students cannot learn effectively in their areas of special need when instructed with regular education methods and materials. The specific process for determining eligibility for special education will be discussed later in this chapter.

Special education is for youngsters with *educational* disabilities. It is not for children with physical disabilities unless those disabilities impede their school performance. The key here is the student's ability to learn in a regular classroom setting.

The following paragraphs describe characteristics that may warrant special education. Consult your state's special education code for the definitions of specific educational disabilities used in your state.

Learning Disability

The term *learning disability* is difficult to define because it embraces a variety of learning characteristics. Some learning-disabled children have a disability restricted to reading (which may be further limited to a problem in the decoding of words or in comprehension). Others—a smaller number—are hampered in their ability to perform mathematical calculations or to reason mathematically. Others have a severe problem with written expression, either the mechanical task of writing or the organization and expression of ideas. And still others may have an attention disorder, meaning that their inability to sustain attention impedes their mastery of academic skills. This is by no means an exhaustive description; in fact, learning disabilities have been identified in such areas as perception, memory, listening, speaking, motor skills, and social skills. Many children with learning disabilities do not "outgrow" their disabilities, but rather continue to experience learning problems into adulthood.

Many experts say that children should not be called learning-disabled unless the following conditions are met: their academic achievement falls significantly below their demonstrated intellectual ability; the learning problem is not attributable to mental retardation, sensory impairment, emotional difficulties, or environmental factors; and they have had appropriate educational opportunities. Definitions—and there are many—typically focus on a language or perceptual difficulty which is presumed to underlie the learning problem.

Communication Disorder

Children may be impaired in their ability to communicate because of a problem in their speech or in their ability to use language effectively. Children with speech problems may have difficulty in articulation (the most common type of communication disorder), voice characteristics (for example, pitch), or fluency (for example, stuttering). Children with language disorders may have difficulty in oral expression or understanding relative to their agemates. Children with communication disorders typically have more than one kind of speech or language problem.

Mental Retardation

Children are considered mentally retarded if their intellectual ability is significantly below average *and* they have difficulties with adaptive behavior, that is, dealing effectively with the social requirements of their environment. This two-part definition recognizes that children who perform very poorly on standardized intelligence tests should not be considered mentally retarded if they function appropriately to their age in social settings.

A number of classification systems have been used to describe the severity of the retardation. The following categories, ranging from least to most severe, are frequently used in educational settings:

educable mentally retarded (EMR)
trainable mentally retarded (TMR)
severely/profoundly mentally retarded

Behavioral or Emotional Problems

Children with behavioral or emotional problems act in a consistently inappropriate way—for their age and for their situation. They often exhibit conflict with their peers or school authority figures, emotional distress, and poor academic performance. Behavior may vary considerably from student to student: some may provoke their peers and defy adults; others may withdraw. Because all children act inappropriately on occasion, it takes training and experience to differentiate between those whose behavior falls within the typical range and those whose behavior qualifies as an educational disability which warrants special education.

Hearing Impairment

A child with a hearing impairment can have a hearing loss ranging from mild to profound. The student may be categorized as deaf, meaning that the loss of hearing is so severe that alternate means of communication (such as sign language) must be used; or hard-of-hearing, meaning that the child can, despite a hearing loss, understand oral speech and may use a hearing aid. The educational modifications and instructional methods vary considerably depending on the level of loss, which is generally measured in decibels.

Visual Impairment

Some students have limited vision to the extent that special provisions are needed for effective learning. This includes students who are totally blind or can only perceive light so that reading must be done with braille; it also includes students who are partially sighted but can only read large-print materials.

Physical Disability

Physical disabilities encompass a wide spectrum of orthopedic or other health problems such as cerebral palsy, spina bifida, juvenile diabetes, epilepsy, and muscular dystrophy. Physically disabled students are eligible for special education when regular education methods need to be substantially modified to meet their educational needs. The school district may also need to adapt the building (for instance, by providing ramps or nonskid surfaces) to allow easy access for the physically disabled. Special equipment, such as book holders, may be required to facilitate learning.

Multiple Handicap

Some severely disabled students have more than one disability: for example, a blind, cerebral-palsied child, or a deaf, mentally retarded child. Frequently excluded from public school programs in the past, children with multiple disabilities are today legally entitled to a full-time public education. The severity of their disabling condition typically requires complex educational planning, with the instructional focus usually placed on the development of social, self-care, and language skills.

Giftedness

Gifted students demonstrate exceptional ability or potential in such areas as intellectual or academic ability, the visual or performing arts, or leadership. The gifted do not fall within the scope of Public Law 94–142; states are therefore under no obligation to provide specialized programs for them as they are for the "handicapped." They are in-

cluded in this listing, however, because they sometimes require specially designed instruction to be challenged commensurate with their
ability. Many states do meet this need by providing such services as
enrichment activities in the regular classroom, resource room programs, summer school, special classes, or even special schools.

Terminology

A word about terms: in attempting to distinguish among different
types of disability, special education professionals have created virtually a new language. But because they have been largely unable to
agree on a uniform terminology, they may apply many terms to a single characteristic or disability. One researcher, for example, counted
thirty-eight terms used to describe the syndrome of minimal brain
dysfunction. Other terms are used without precision; the same term
may mean different things to different people. *Dyslexia*, for example,
is often used freely to refer to a wide range of learning problems. In
so doing, specialists often confuse each other, not to mention the parents and classroom teachers with whom they work.

But parents and educators must talk to each other, so what is a
parent to do? Until precise terminology is agreed upon, you can most
effectively communicate with specialists by talking about your child
in terms of observable behaviors (she fidgets; he mixes up letters when
he reads) and avoiding recourse to jargon or labels (she is hyperactive; he is dyslexic). When you want to use a special term, explain how
you are using it so that you can be sure that you and the specialist are
on the same wavelength. If the specialist uses a term, do not hesitate
to ask for clarification even if you think you know what it means, and
even if you think you are supposed to know what it means.

THE SPECIAL EDUCATION PROCESS

While the process by which a child with an educational disability
is identified, evaluated, and provided with an educational program
varies somewhat from state to state and district to district, federal requirements dictate a general sequence of steps. Figure 1.1 illustrates
this sequence. This flow chart indicates some of the points at which
you as parent can appeal a school's action or recommendation; in fact,
you can appeal at any point of the process.   (Appeal procedures are
discussed in depth in Chapter 7.) Each step is discussed below. Subsequent chapters more fully describe the evaluation and IEP process.

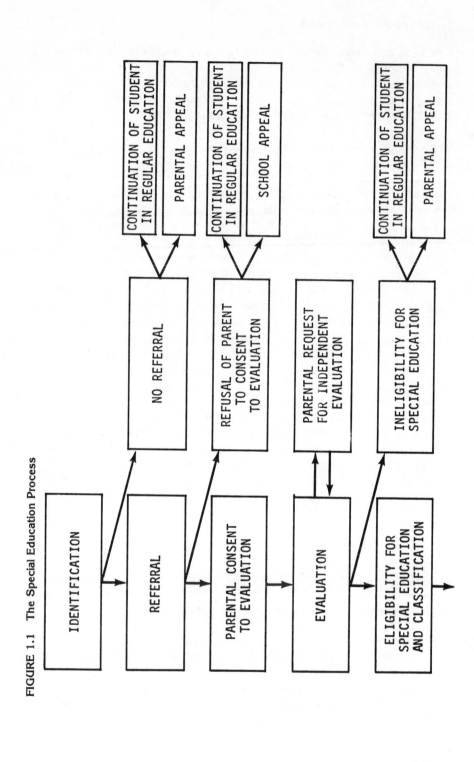

FIGURE 1.1 The Special Education Process

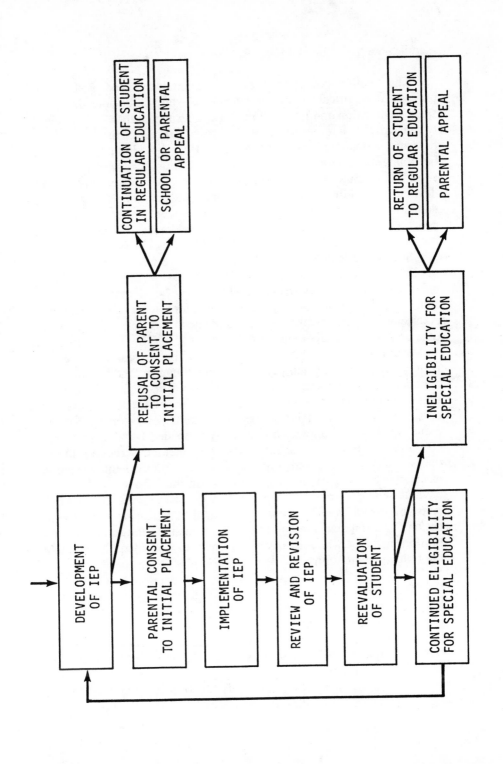

Identification

The identification stage is the entry point of the special education process. It is critical because it determines who will be considered for special education and who will not. It can also spell the difference between early or late detection of a learning problem; early identification and educational intervention can keep a learning problem from becoming more serious and minimize frustration later. For these reasons, Public Law 94–142 obligates states and local school districts to develop "child-find" programs to identify all minors who may have educational disabilities—from birth to age twenty-one—within their geographical areas. Such programs are not limited to public schools, but must encompass private schools and institutions as well.

States and local districts must make active efforts to apprise the public of the evaluative and educational services available for students who have special needs. Children may be identified as having school-related difficulties by parents, principals, teachers, guidance counselors, nurses, doctors, judges, and social service workers, among others. School districts may use a variety of information sources to screen for special education candidates, including standardized test results, teachers' judgment, classroom performance, and parents' perceptions. While they may seek parents' input, districts can carry out these preliminary screening procedures without consulting the parents. (Don't confuse this "screening" with the later step of preplacement "evaluation" for which your okay is needed.)

Most school districts have rather regimented screening procedures that draw on various types and sources of information. Parents can nevertheless play an important role in identifying children who have disabilities. Appendix A provides a list of warning signs that may help you decide whether your child would benefit from further evaluation. You can start the ball rolling by bringing to the school's attention problems of which it may not be aware. Consider, for example, the following situations:

The child is too young to be enrolled in a regular public school.

The parents observe difficulties at home that suggest a learning problem.

The screening procedures stress educational areas in which the student performs well and neglects areas in which the student is deficient.

The teacher is reluctant to identify children in general, or has dismissed a disability as laziness or lack of motivation.

The child has not been identified because there is already a waiting list of children to be evaluated.
A child with learning problems is passive in class and is therefore
  neglected in favor of a more disruptive student.
A secondary school child has several teachers, none of whom
  spends enough time with the student to recognize a learning
  problem.

If you believe that your child may need special education services, the
next section tells you how to request an evaluation.

Referral

Once the identification process is complete, and children who are
experiencing learning or behavior problems have been brought to the
school's attention, school officials (usually a building principal or a
committee of district educators) consider the needs of each child and
determine which students, as probable candidates for special education services, will be referred for evaluation, and which will not. If a
school district has decided not to refer your child, he or she may still
be eligible for regular education services such as a remedial reading
program or the assistance of a guidance counselor. You may challenge a school's decision not to refer your child through due-process
procedures.

If your child is referred for evaluation, a school official (usually
the teacher or principal) completes a referral form describing the reason for the referral. The school contacts you, asking you to come in
for a meeting or explaining the situation in a letter. Public Law 94–142
requires school officials to give you in writing—in your native language—the reason for the referral, a description of the evaluation
process and procedures, and a listing of legal safeguards available to
you. A school official, typically the principal, must now request your
written consent. Your consent at this point only authorizes the school
district to evaluate your child; placement in a special education program is a separate step requiring further consent.

Your meeting with school staff has another less tangible but
equally important goal: laying the groundwork for a cooperative relationship between home and school. A session in which school staff do
all the talking and parents do all the listening defeats this purpose. You
should take this opportunity to share useful information about your
child, ask questions, clarify terms, and relate concerns. You may well
be able to offer suggestions about the evaluation itself, since you best

know how your child might react to a particular approach, or to such factors as the time of day or the setting in which the evaluation takes place. You might want to discuss how the evaluation should be presented to your child. The special education maze, with its many procedures and its jargon, takes time to master, so do not hesitate to ask seemingly obvious questions or to ask for clarification of any issue.

You can request a referral for evaluation. While a school district is not obligated to honor your request, it must at least review your child's educational status and determine whether he or she is likely to be educationally disabled. If so, the district must conduct the evaluation; if not, the district may refuse your request although it must inform you in writing of its reasons.

If you are considering requesting an evaluation of your child, follow the steps described below:

• Gather information on your child's learning and behavioral characteristics by talking with the teacher, reviewing records and work samples, and carefully observing your child's approach to learning tasks. Consider whether your child's skills and characteristics seem to differ significantly from those expected of children of the same age and whether your child appears to have a specific learning problem. Experienced teachers can be excellent sources for information about age- and grade-level norms. The appendix contains a list of "warning signs" that may help you spot a possible educational disability. You can also consult your local library to find age profiles. (See *For Further Information* at the end of this chapter.)

• After gathering this information, try working with the teacher to address any problems your child is having in the classroom.

• If your child continues to show signs of an educational disability and you believe special education is warranted, write a letter to the school principal, with a copy to the director of special education or special services, requesting a referral for evaluation. A written request generally sparks action faster than a spoken request. Figure 1.2 provides a sample letter that you can copy or adapt.

• If the school district does not respond to the letter within three weeks, call or send a follow-up letter to the principal or the director of special education or special services.

• If the school district refuses your request, it must explain its reasons in writing. You can contest this decision at a due-process

FIGURE 1.2   Sample Letter Requesting a Referral for Evaluation

Linda and Bradd Riley
969 Morton Street
Fairview, Indiana 46123

November 3, 1986

Ms. Elaine Howard, Principal
Lyncrest Elementary School
Fairview, Indiana 46123

Dear Ms. Howard:

We are the parents of Janet Riley, a student in Mr. Phillips' second grade. We are writing to request that Janet be referred for evaluation to the district's evaluation team to determine whether she is eligible for special education and related services.

Janet was eight years old last February. She has had difficulty keeping up with her classmates academically since early in first grade. She continued to have problems last year despite her diligent efforts, accommodations made by her teacher (Ms. Blackwell), and our reinforcement of the teacher's lessons. In addition, Janet received extra help in reading through the school's remedial program. Janet's performance on the California Achievement Tests at the end of last year showed her reading skills overall were at the fourth percentile and math skills were at the eleventh percentile, when compared with other first graders nationwide.

We talked with Ms. Blackwell in June about the possibility of retention but decided that this would not be a good solution, since Janet was already older and taller than most of her classmates. This year Janet has continued to have academic problems. In addition, we are seeing signs of frustration and discouragement that were not evident last year. Mr. Phillips has been sensitive to Janet's difficulties and has made adjustments in his instruction for which we are appreciative, but Janet's learning problems have persisted.

We are concerned that Janet's learning problems are continuing and her resistance to school is growing. We are therefore eager for an evaluation to be conducted as soon as possible so that, with the school staff, we can have a clearer picture of Janet's learning problem and determine whether special education is warranted. We are willing to contribute to this process in whatever way you think will be helpful.

Thank you. We look forward to hearing from you.

Sincerely,

Linda E. Riley   *Bradd Riley*

Linda Eckert Riley   Bradd Riley

cc: Dr. Scott Newland
Director of Special Services

hearing. If you choose to do this, the school district must tell you how to initiate such a hearing.

• You can obtain a professional evaluation at your own expense. If you do, the school district must review and consider the results.

Evaluation

The evaluation must be conducted by a multidisciplinary team using a variety of information sources and must be completed before your child can be given special education services. State regulations may require that an evaluation be completed and an eligibility decision made within a specified number of days after parental consent is obtained. If you are dissatisfied with any aspect of the school's evaluation, you may request an independent evaluation. Chapter 2 delves further into the evaluation process.

Eligibility Determination and Classification

School staff use the evaluation results to determine whether your child qualifies for special education and to pinpoint the educational needs to be used in developing an appropriate program. In most states, a student is declared eligible for special education when: (1) he or she is determined to have a specific educationally handicapping condition, resulting in the assignment of a formal classification (for example, "communication handicapped"); and (2) special education is determined to be necessary to meet the student's educational needs. The intent of these criteria is to limit special education to students who have a specific and identifiable problem of a cognitive, emotional, or physical nature that is impairing their educational performance.

You find out about the results of the school's evaluation and the eligibility decision either in a letter or at a meeting. In some districts, this may be the same meeting at which the Individualized Education Program (IEP) is developed; in other districts, two separate meetings are held.

The school district must let you in on the evaluation results even when it finds that your child does not need special education. You will probably have questions at this point. What other steps might be taken to help your child learn more effectively? Would tutoring, or a schedule change, or participation in extracurricular activities make sense? What light do the evaluation results shed on how you can best deal with your child at home? Should you consider counseling for the child or for the family? If you disagree with the ineligibility decision, remember that you can challenge it.

In most states, students qualify for special education only if they are formally classified as having a specific educational disability in accordance with the state's classification system. In effect, they must be labeled to receive services. These classification categories attempt to group together students with similar learning problems to facilitate the development of appropriate educational programs. The specific classification often guides placement decisions. These categories are defined in state regulations; specialized evaluations are sometimes required before a classification can be assigned. Indiana's classification categories, listed below, typify those used by many states:

communication handicapped
emotionally handicapped
hearing impaired
learning disabled
mentally handicapped
multiply handicapped
physically handicapped
visually handicapped

Few educational issues have generated more controversy or aroused more emotion than the classification, or labeling, of children receiving special education. The issue merited a wide-ranging study, initiated in 1972 by then Secretary of Health, Education, and Welfare Elliot Richardson, of the classification of children and its potential abuses. The study was conducted under the leadership of prominent educator Nicholas Hobbs, who summarized its results in *The Futures of Children*. Hobbs stressed that the classification systems typically used to categorize special education students are vulnerable to serious abuses; nevertheless, he concluded that some form of classification was necessary to ensure the provision of appropriate services.

Classification continues to spark controversy. Indeed, some states such as Massachusetts have abandoned use of traditional categories altogether and instead require only a designation of "in need of special education" to qualify for specialized instruction. Parents as well as educators must be vocal in the ongoing debate. Whatever system is used, we must remember that no classification can substitute for an in-depth understanding of the "whole" child, and that the ultimate aim is to match students and their unique learning characteristics with appropriate educational programs.

Development of the IEP

Once the school finds that your son or daughter qualifies for special education, an IEP team must meet within thirty calendar days to construct an Individualized Education Program, including the special education placement. You are part of the IEP team, and so is your child if that is appropriate. (A meeting to develop the IEP may only be held without you if the school district has made a serious effort to get you to participate.) Together with other members of the team—school or district staff—you plan an Individualized Education Program, including the special education placement.

How active you are in the process depends on many factors, but in any case the school district must obtain your written consent before it can put into effect this initial special education placement. If you withhold consent, the district may either terminate the process altogether, in which case your child cannot receive special education services, or it may appeal your decision.

Implementation of the IEP

Once you give your consent, the school district must implement the IEP as soon as possible. The precise manner in which the IEP is implemented is a critical factor in the success of the special education program and requires careful planning by school staff and parents.

Review of the IEP

You share responsibility with the special education teacher and other school staff for monitoring your child's progress and ensuring that the IEP continues to meet his or her needs. Public Law 94–142 requires that the IEP be formally reviewed by the IEP team at least annually, although you or the school may request a review before it is scheduled. This review may result in revision of the program described in the IEP (for example, a change in the special education placement) or in the continuation of the same educational services described in the previous IEP.

Reevaluation

Public Law 94–142 requires that school districts reevaluate all special education students at least once every three years, or more often if judged necessary by the school or requested by parents. (Some states require more frequent reevaluation.) The reevaluation determines whether your child continues to qualify for special education. If the answer is no (a decision that you can appeal), your child is "declassified" and receives only regular education services. If the answer is yes, the IEP team meets again (with you as a member) to revise the IEP according to the reevaluation findings.

A FINAL NOTE

Special education in the United States has come a long way since its advent in the last century. To appreciate the dramatic changes that have taken place, we might look back to a case decided in 1919: in *Beattie* v. *State Board of Education*, the Wisconsin Supreme Court ruled that a child with cerebral palsy could be denied a public school education "because of his depressing and nauseating effect on the teachers and schoolchildren and . . . [because] he required an undue portion of the teacher's time."

While we have traveled far on the road to a free appropriate public education for all children who have educational disabilities, the journey is not over. The legal machinery is in place to help translate the promise of equal educational opportunity into reality, yet legislation, no matter how sweeping, cannot alone meet this goal. Compliance with the letter of the law does not ensure that its spirit, or ultimate purpose, will also be achieved—just as the development of an IEP that meets legal requirements does not ensure that your child will actually receive an appropriate educational program.

The success of our efforts to educate *all* children effectively hinges on many factors, including sufficient governmental funds, adequate facilities and resources, and properly trained staff in adequate numbers. A less tangible requirement may be the linchpin to success: a change in our way of thinking about students with disabilities. Public Law 94–142 challenges us to view them as young people who, if provided with appropriate educational programs, are capable of learning—often on a par with other students—and as potentially productive members of society.

The law also appeals to educators and parents to view each other as partners in the educational process. As this cognitive shift takes place, and as parents continue to expand their involvement in special education, the way will be paved for the provision of appropriate educational programs for all children.

FOR FURTHER INFORMATION

Copies of Public Law 94–142 and the implementing regulations can be obtained by writing to Special Education Programs, Room 3527, Switzer Building, 330 C Street, S.W., Washington, D.C. 20202.

Copies of Section 504 and the implementing regulations can be obtained by writing to the regional office of the Office for Civil Rights for your state.

State legislation regarding the education of students with special needs is available from your state department of education or your local school district. State and local annual plans for the education of special education students, mandated by Public Law 94–142, are also available to the public.

Elkind, D. (1978). *A sympathetic understanding of the child: Birth to sixteen.* 2d ed. Boston: Allyn and Bacon.

Ilg, F.L. (1981). *Child behavior.* New York: Harper and Row. The above books provide year-by-year profiles of the mental, personal, and social development of children.

Hobbs, N. (1975). *The futures of children.* San Francisco: Jossey-Bass. An excellent discussion of the results and recommendations of a comprehensive study of issues involved in classifying children.

Martin, R. (1979). *Educating handicapped children: The legal mandate.* Champaign, Ill.: Research Press. Written by an attorney well versed in the educational rights of students who have educational disabilities, this book reviews the events leading up to the passage of Public Law 94–142 and interprets its provisions in the light of federal regulations and legal decisions.

Yohalem, D., and Dinsmore, J. (1978). *94–142 and 504: Numbers that add up to educational rights for handicapped children.* Washington, D.C.: Children's Defense Fund. A basic primer on federal special education legislation, written with parents in mind. (See Appendix B for publisher's address.)

The following is a sampling of introductory textbooks on special education. Each contains individual chapters on the different educationally disabling conditions.

Haring, N. G., ed. (1982). *Exceptional children and youth.* 3d ed. Columbus, Ohio: Charles E. Merrill.

Kirk, S. A., and Gallagher, J. J. (1983). *Educating exceptional children.* 4th ed. Boston: Houghton Mifflin.

Meyen, E. L., ed. (1982). *Exceptional children and youth—An intro-
    duction*. 2d ed. Denver: Love.
Payne, J. S., and Kauffman, J. M. (1983). *Exceptional children in fo-
    cus*. Columbus, Ohio: Charles E. Merrill.

2

The Evaluation Process

David is like many other first graders: he is finding it difficult to learn to read. David's problems did not surface this year; in fact, he is repeating first grade. His teacher recommended his retention last spring because David's performance revealed gaps in the development of his "reading readiness"—skills a child needs in order to learn to read. She thought that particularly in view of his age (he was born in December, and was therefore younger than most of his classmates), another year in first grade would give him time to catch up, and would avoid almost certain frustration and failure in the second grade.

David's second year in first grade began on a promising note. He was already familiar with classroom routines and early in the fall emerged as a leader to whom other children sometimes looked for direction. Placement in the top math group and the middle reading group at the outset of the year also boosted his self-confidence. The discomfort of the previous year, when he had been painfully aware of being the slowest reader in the class, began to fade.

David's surge of confidence was short-lived, however. By October's end, his reading performance faltered as particular skills posed problems: he was finding it difficult to grasp the rules of phonics, and words that he seemed to know one week would elude him the next. Reluctantly, David's teacher moved him into the lower reading group. At the same time, she referred him to the school's remedial reading teacher who arranged to work with him twice a week in a small-group setting.

Now sensitive to his possible learning disability, David's teacher began to note other weaknesses. David was sometimes inattentive and frequently would need to have directions or explanations repeated. Also, printing was proving a struggle for him, particularly when he was asked to copy from the blackboard. David began to show signs of frustration and discouragement as he became increasingly aware of how his academic problems separated him from his classmates. He became reluctant to attend the remedial reading program, sometimes refusing to go at all.

Toward the end of November, the classroom teacher, who had occasionally spoken with David's parents by telephone, met with them to discuss her concerns about David's scant progress in reading. Her report distressed his parents, who had hoped that retention would resolve David's academic difficulties. They told the teacher that they had also observed some changes in their son in the last month: for example, he had become increasingly resistant to going to school in the morning. This came as no surprise to the teacher, since David had become a frequent visitor to the school nurse, complaining of stomachaches.

The following week David's teacher met with the principal and the school social worker. After carefully reviewing David's educational history, current academic status, and steps taken to help him in the classroom, they initiated a referral for evaluation by the district's evaluation team. The parents were called in a few days later. After being informed of the reasons for the referral, the evaluation procedures, the possible outcomes, and their due-process rights, and after discussing some of their concerns about what all of this might mean for David and for them, they gave written consent to the evaluation.

PARENTS' CONCERNS ABOUT THE EVALUATION

Most parents anticipate the evaluation of their child for a possible educational disability with mixed emotions. You as a parent may feel relief that a team of professionals will finally tell you why your child is not learning as easily as other people's children, or like your own other children. At the same time, you may be fraught with anxiety about what the evaluation will show.

As the parent of a child who has learning problems, you may be a long-time rider on an emotional roller coaster. Parents in this position often describe their experience as exasperating, overwhelming, frantic, sometimes hopeful, but usually bewildering. A school meeting like the one David's parents attended to discuss an evaluation of their child understandably touches off—all at once or in an exhausting sequence—many responses, including some of these:

Denial: Not my child!
Rage: The school should have picked this up long ago.

Blame: If only I hadn't gone back to work so soon.

Worry: Will he ever learn to read? Will she ever be able to support herself?

Guilt: Where did I go wrong?

Hope: Maybe it's just a stage.

Relief: Finally they're going to do something.

Given time and reliable information, this sorting-out process usually leads to a more realistic acceptance of the situation ("He may always find reading a chore, but he remembers almost everything people say to him").

Relief may well dominate your reaction, for a referral for evaluation often validates parents' own concerns about their child's difficulties. Perhaps, like many parents, you have long suspected that your child has learning problems; perhaps, like many others, you have been dissuaded from pursuing an evaluation by family or friends or by well-meaning professionals. A pediatrician may have suggested that Frankie is just "all boy," more interested in romping than reading. A psychologist may have recommended a wait-and-see approach to determine whether your child's difficulty stems from simple immaturity—a "maturational lag," in educational jargon. Or a teacher may have assured you that extra help or another year in the same grade would solve the problem. While these recommendations are no doubt appropriate for some children some of the time, for others they only delay identification and remediation of specific learning problems.

At this point, relief may give rise to unrealistic expectations about what the evaluation will accomplish. You may be assuming that a school-based evaluation is something like a medical procedure: the professionals will do some testing, diagnose the source of the problem, offer a clear prognosis, and prescribe the educational cure. Once the evaluation team focuses attention on the child, you may —like many parents—express high hopes: "Now we'll get to the root of the problem," or "Finally we'll get some answers." Realism is important here. Evaluations certainly provide some answers, but they rarely offer the kind of straightforward explanations that you are probably hoping to hear.

The evaluation may also stir a number of fears or anxieties. You may worry that it will confirm your worst fears: that Diane will never be able to read, that Jimmy will be found to be retarded, or that Paul has little chance of ever becoming self-sufficient. In some cases such fears are well founded; most often, they are not. Of the many children evaluated for learning problems, a distinct minority are found to be mentally retarded. And it is the rare individual who, with appropriate instruction, cannot learn to read at the sixth-grade level.

More likely your child will be found to have average or near-average intellectual ability, with a learning disorder in specific skill areas. With appropriate educational programs, your child will in all likelihood make reasonable academic gains, or will develop ways of coping with or compensating for the disability. Many people have compensated successfully for a learning disability—not always in the remarkable fashion that Nelson Rockefeller, Bruce Jenner, and Winston Churchill compensated for theirs, but well enough to lead fulfilling, productive lives.

The evaluation team may recommend a change in your child's educational program, and this too can provoke anxiety. You may think that by consenting to the evaluation, you are relinquishing your role in the decision-making process. You may fear that school officials will place your child in a grossly inappropriate educational setting, leaving him or her there year after year with little monitoring. Such abuses undoubtedly occurred in the past, when parents had little or no involvement in the special education process; of course, such abuse may still occur, but it is illegal, and the law gives you options for preventing or remedying an improper placement. Public Law 94–142 includes a series of requirements which all public school districts are required to follow, including the mandate that the district place the special education student in the "least restrictive environment" and that the district obtain the written consent of parents before the initial special education program can be implemented. The bottom line is that the school is legally bound to involve you in virtually every step of the special education process, and that impartial third-party resolution is available when you and the school system are in conflict.

PREPARING FOR THE EVALUATION

If you have concerns about the evaluation and its possible consequences, you might arrange to speak with school officials or other professionals, or to other parents. Such school staff members as school psychologists, learning disabilities specialists, social workers, and guidance counselors can be particularly helpful in explaining the evaluation process. You may also want to offer suggestions about the evaluation that will help your child to do his or her best: "Cecily is more alert in the morning." "Tommy's been upset because his pet hamster died; it's probably better not to mention pets." "Ralph doesn't like to wear his new glasses, he sometimes hides them in his lunch-box.''

A number of parent and professional groups can provide information and support, including the Association for Children with Learning Disabilities (ACLD) and the Council for Exceptional Children (CEC), both of which have local chapters throughout the country. You'll find addresses of their national headquarters in the appendix. Talking to other parents whose children have been evaluated can be helpful and reassuring. There may be a special education Parent-Teacher Association (often abbreviated as SEPTA) in your district that can provide contacts.

Like many parents, you may fear that the evaluation itself will make your child more self-conscious about a learning difficulty, or that it will have social repercussions by singling out your child in school, or that the testing process will be just one more experience with failure and frustration. These fears may be legitimate; more often they are unfounded. Certainly many children are apprehensive about being called out of class for testing by an unfamiliar adult, but this anxiety usually abates as the examiner puts the child at ease: members of the evaluation team are trained, and usually experienced, at doing just that. They usually know how to establish rapport, dispel fears, elicit optimal responses, and minimize frustration. And many of the evaluative tasks are not threatening. Figuring out what letter a neurologist has drawn on your back, for example, can be intriguing, and trying to toss a beanbag through a hole can be fun. Some of the more school-related tasks, such as defining words, reading short passages, or solving math problems, may be less pleasant, especially if they tap an area of weakness. You might remind your child that they won't be graded on these tasks, that the point is for the school to find out what kind of help they can give.

A child who is summoned from class for testing is unavoidably singled out, but this may not be as awkward or embarrassing for your child as you imagine. Most public schools offer a range of "pull-out" programs or services so that children are frequently called out of the regular class for a variety of reasons: Joe leaves the room for speech therapy; Marsha for a saxophone lesson; Jason for remedial reading. A note summoning your child from class is an ordinary part of the school day and will probably cause little stir.

Testing does call attention to the learning problem, but your daughter or son is probably already aware of having difficulty. The separation of children into hierarchical groups starts as early as first grade when reading groups are formed. However, the evaluation need not undermine or discourage your child. Ideally, it provides an opportunity for the evaluator to offer reassurance and to mention that many students, including some very "smart" children, have learning problems in some areas, and that there are ways to help them. In short, an appropriate evaluation does not usually leave any lasting negative impressions on the child. Some children are actually disappointed when the evaluation ends and it's time to return to class. They are sometimes eager to see the evaluator again, and are usually pleased to be greeted in the corridor by their new acquaintance.

Nevertheless, it is important that you prepare your child for the evaluation and help relieve anxieties by discussing it several days before it is scheduled to begin. This is best done in an open, straightforward, calm manner, in language that your child will readily understand. Keep in mind that you could, through subtle cues, unintentionally convey your own anxieties about the evaluation; children, including those with learning disabilities, are often expert at reading such cues. For this reason you may want to speak with someone else—spouse, friend, or professional—to dispel your own worries about the situation before presenting it to your child. You might even do a dry run before this discussion. Of course you have your own style of talking things over with your son or daughter, but here is an example of what you might say to an elementary school child with a reading problem:

> David, I know you've been having a hard time with reading. Remember I talked to your teacher last week? Well, we'd like to help you learn to read better. So some people who work at your school— they're kind of like special teachers—they're going to work with you for a few days next week. It'll take about an hour each day. They're going to find out why you're having trouble reading and how the school can help you. One of the people you'll be seeing is Dr. Altman. You've probably seen her around school. She's a psychologist who has worked with a lot of kids in your school who have trouble with reading, and she's been able to help them learn better. So, what do you think? How do you feel about it?

Give your child a chance to ask questions or express fears about the evaluation. If there's not much immediate reaction, wait a day or so and ask again. Children may or may not verbalize the following kinds of questions:

> Will I be left back?
> Will I stay at the same school? In the same class?
> Will I get grades on the tests?

What happens if I miss my spelling test?
Will I miss lunch? Recess?
Do the other kids know? What should I tell them?
Is this the kind of doctor that gives shots?

By anticipating (but not prompting) these concerns, you can be both reassuring and realistic. Once the evaluation has been completed, you will want to talk it over with your child so that you can hear about any reactions and especially any resulting fears or anxieties.

THE EVALUATION RESULTS:
WHAT YOU WILL AND WON'T LEARN

To most people, evaluation means testing. But the evaluation of a child with learning problems should encompass much more than the administration of tests. A school-based evaluation assembles data from a variety of sources, including tests, to guide decisions about a child's educational program. Its ultimate aim is to provide information that can be used to help a student strengthen academic skills and to prepare him or her for a productive life after leaving school. Merely assessing a problem and assigning a classification, without providing a child with appropriate help, is not sufficient.

You may think that evaluation seeks primarily to detect the cause of a learning problem; this is a common misconception. The etiology, or cause, is typically more elusive than you expect. A multitude of factors—hereditary, neurological, biochemical, nutritional, environmental, motivational, emotional, social, and so on—may contribute to an educational disability, but only in rare cases can a single cause be isolated. For example, a learning-disabled child who has a neurological impairment stemming from birth complications may also suffer from low self-esteem. This "I-can't-do-it" syndrome may impede academic progress as much as the learning disability. Occasionally a learning problem may be traced to a specific event; for example, head trauma or lead poisoning may cause neurological damage and associated learning difficulties. Most often, evaluators can reach only speculative conclusions about the roots of a learning problem, but can more confidently pinpoint current factors that are aggravating the problem.

Why go ahead with an evaluation if it won't tell you why your child is having difficulties in school? In the first place, the "why" is often less important than you think. Establishing cause doesn't necessarily tell you or the school how to help your child. For example, determining that Ronnie has "minimal brain dysfunction" provides virtually no guidance to you or to the teacher about instructional strategies. On the other hand, knowing that he has mastered basic addition and subtraction facts but is unable to add multidigit numbers that require regrouping gives the teacher useful data with which to address Ronnie's problems.

In the second place, cause is not destiny. Just as we cannot always identify with certainty the root of a learning problem, we cannot predict with complete confidence the course it will take. Every professional working with children who have educational disabilities can point to students who have made dramatic and unexpected educational gains, as well as to students who are treading water academically despite intensive and varied special education instruction.

EVALUATION: A TEAM APPROACH

A team of professionals, rather than a single individual, can best evaluate a child with learning problems. Indeed, Public Law 94-142 mandates that a *multidisciplinary* team—that is, a team whose members have expertise in different professional areas—conduct the evaluation. If one individual is solely responsible for your child's evaluation, the school is not complying with the law, even if that individual has a wall covered with credentials.

We have been calling this group the evaluation team, but different districts or states may call its evaluation unit by different names: a school-based support team; a special education assessment team; a core evaluation team; a child-study team; an M-team; etc. Each state has specific requirements about the composition of the multidisciplinary team; it may include a school psychologist who conducts a psychological evaluation, a learning specialist or educational diagnostician who conducts an educational evaluation, and a school social worker who conducts a social and family assessment. These professionals usually have to meet specific state requirements to be certified for employment in their fields. The classroom teacher, who has the opportunity to observe your child daily in the natural educational setting, is another key team player.

The school-based group may seek out the opinions of other professionals to provide a more complete picture of your child. A comprehensive evaluation typically also includes a medical examination.

Don't forget that you are also a member of the team that evaluates your child, and that your inclusion in this group is not just a public relations gesture. The law recognizes that parents play a key role in the evaluation process. Unquestionably, no one knows your child as well as you. You can provide essential information regarding your child's medical and developmental history as well as information on day-to-day functioning. Your comments about your child's interests, relationships with family and friends, work habits, and future aspirations can give educators ideas about how best to respond to your child in school.

In addition to assembling information from a variety of professional vantage points, an evaluation team typically gathers data by observing in the classroom, reviewing the student file, consulting with parents and school staff, reviewing classroom work, and testing.

Classroom Observation. Since the classroom experience can dramatically affect a child's educational performance, the evaluation team must assess the learning environment as well as the learner. This observation can provide a wealth of information about your child's interactions with the teacher and classmates, about work habits and possible obstacles to learning, and about alternative approaches to which he or she might respond. An observer might look at the location of your child's seat in the classroom, your youngster's attention to task, activities that pose particular difficulties, level of preparation, participation in class, and verbal and nonverbal interactions. The observer would probably also look at your youngster's reactions in various circumstances: is he or she relaxed, anxious, confused, enthusiastic, frustrated, proud, restless, distracted?

Review of Student File. The school maintains a cumulative file on your child's school career. Reviewing the information it contains may suggest a long-term pattern that warrants exploration: comments by several teachers that Julio often doesn't understand directions may point to hearing problems; a sudden drop in Rachel's attendance or grades may suggest a problem of recent origin—perhaps events at home or in school that are getting in her way. The evaluation team will probably look at this file. Remember that you are part of the team: school officials generally recognize your right, now guaranteed by federal legislation, to review any and all materials in your child's files.

Consultation with Parents and School Staff. As previously mentioned, parents and teachers can provide vital information to the evaluation team. Other people who know your child—school administrators, the nurse, a tutor or therapist, the guidance counselor, even the school secretary—can contribute to an understanding of his or her educational functioning. Previous teachers can also broaden the picture of your child's learning history.

Review of Classroom Work. Samples of your child's classroom work often indicate skill levels, areas of strength and weakness, motivational level, conceptual understanding, and handwriting ability.

Testing. Testing is only one facet of the evaluation process and represents a limited sampling of your child's academic functioning; it is, however, an important way to take stock of educational strengths and weaknesses. The following section explains some basic tenets of testing.

MAKING SENSE OF TEST RESULTS

Hundreds of tests serving a range of purposes are available for the assessment of learning problems. This section briefly describes some of the more significant types of tests used in evaluating children with school-related difficulties. Tests can be administered on a group or individual basis; individually administered tests are usually better geared to evaluating children with a suspected learning disorder and generate more information.

Different types of tests have different aims. An aptitude test estimates a child's overall capacity for learning. An achievement test provides a global estimate of a student's skill level in an academic area. A diagnostic test zooms in for a close-up view of the academic skill area, and indicates strengths, weaknesses, and error patterns. You might ask what types of tests will be given to your child as part of the evaluation process. Bear in mind that a comprehensive evaluation should include aptitude, achievement, and diagnostic tests.

You may also want to ask how the test is scored. Here, too, some background information is helpful. Some tests, such as intelligence tests, are norm-referenced: the score is a number that compares your child's performance to that of a large sample of children of the same age. (The sample is called the standardization sample, and the type of test scored this way is often called a standardized test.) Other tests are criterion-referenced: the results take the form of an inventory of specific skills that your child has or has not mastered. Whatever form the test results take, keep in mind that tests provide an estimate—not an absolute and fixed measure—of a child's skills and abilities.

Test results typically are expressed in one of the following kinds of scores:

Intelligence Quotient (IQ): Score on an intelligence test where 100 is the norm.

Mental Age (MA): A score, given as an age (for example, 6 years 9 months) that tells you that your child has performed at a level that is typical for a student of that age.

Grade-Level Equivalent: A score, given as a grade (for example, 5.4, the fourth month of the fifth grade) that tells you that your child has performed at a level that is typical for a student at that grade level.

Percentile: A score, given as a number (for example, the 45th percentile) that tells you that your child has performed at a level equal to or better than a particular percentage of the standardization sample. A child who scores at the 45th percentile performed as well as or better than 45 out of every 100 students in the sample. The percentile can be national—in which case your child's score is compared to those of children across the country—or local—in which case your child's score is compared with those of children in your state or community.

Stanine: A standard score, ranging from a low of 1 to a high of 9, with an average score of 5.

Profile of Skills: Not a quantitative score, but rather a descriptive account of skills that your child has or has not mastered.

Tests provide a store of information about your child's approach to learning tasks that is not reflected in the score. The evaluator who observes the testing can find out a great deal about your child's strengths and weaknesses, ability to focus attention, creativity, ability to reflect, and preferred modes of learning—in short, about your child's learning style. This information may be as relevant as test scores in developing teaching strategies that will help your child.

The overriding principle that should guide assessment of all children is: how can this information be used to help the child? This seemingly self-evident question can be easily forgotten. Tests do not exist to generate scores or to produce labels, but to provide information on specific strengths and weaknesses that suggests how and where to work with the child. You should not be content with obtaining information about the nature of the problem, but should press to find out, in concrete terms, how you can use this information to help your child at home and what instructional programs are available in school to address the specific needs identified by the evaluation.

EVALUATION: THE LEGAL REQUIREMENTS

Because the evaluation can have such a significant impact on your child's educational experiences and opportunities, and because it is vulnerable to abuse, the framers of Public Law 94–142 included explicit regulations to guide evaluators in assessing children with learning problems. The thrust of these regulations is to provide a comprehensive, individualized, unbiased assessment that is subject to periodic review.

SUMMARY OF ASSESSMENT REGULATIONS

• Your written consent is required before a school district can conduct a preplacement evaluation of your child.
• The evaluation is conducted to determine whether your child has an educational disability and, if so, to identify an appropriate educational program. The evaluation must therefore take place *before* your child can be placed in a special education program.
• The evaluation must be individually administered and must go beyond the standard testing procedures used with all students in the district.
• The evaluation must be conducted by trained persons in accordance with published instructions regarding administration and scoring.
• The evaluation must be conducted by a multidisciplinary team of professionals, at least one of whom is knowledgeable in the area of the suspected disability.
• The evaluation team must assess, in the language of Public Law 94–142, "all areas related to the suspected disability, including, where appropriate, health, vision, hearing, social and emotional status, general intelligence, academic performance, communicative status, and motor abilities." A complete testing battery is not required as long as the suspected disability is thoroughly assessed; for example, a child referred for evaluation because of a speech-articulation problem need not receive a psychological evaluation.
• The tests and other evaluation procedures must be valid for the purposes they serve.

• The tests must be chosen and administered so that the results accurately reflect what the test is intended to measure, and so that the outcome is not affected by weaknesses in sensory, motor, or communication skills (unless the test is designed to measure those skills). For example, a student with a suspected hearing problem should not be judged to have poor conceptual skills on the basis of an oral test.

• The evaluation procedures and materials must be in your child's native language or normal mode of oral and written communication, if feasible. This might be braille for a blind student or sign language for a deaf student. (For some bilingual students, the normal mode of oral communication might be one language while the normal mode of written communication might be another.)

• The evaluation procedures and materials must not be racially or culturally discriminatory.

• The evaluation must assess your child's specific educational needs; it is inappropriate to give the same battery of tests to all students who are referred for evaluation. The evaluation must not be limited to identifying an IQ score.

• The placement decision must be based on information from a variety of sources and must not derive solely from the results of a single procedure (for example, an IQ test).

• If your child is found to have an educational disability, he or she must be reevaluated every three years (or more often if necessary), or if you or a teacher request it.

• If you disagree with the school district's evaluation of your child, you have the right to a second opinion. You can request an independent evaluation in a letter to the superintendent of the school district or to the director of special education or special services.

THE INDEPENDENT EVALUATION: A SECOND OPINION

Will you foot the bill for the second opinion? Not necessarily. The school district cannot simply refuse to pay for it. It must either pay for an independent evaluation by appropriate professionals or challenge your request by initiating a due-process hearing. If the hearing officer decides that the original evaluation was appropriate, the school district does not have to pay for a second opinion; however, if the hearing officer finds the original evaluation to be inappropriate or questionable, the school district must pick up the tab.

Of course, you can always choose to obtain an independent evaluation at your own expense. And it may be covered by your health insurance policy. But if the school is off the hook, and you are acting on your own, where do you start? Back at the school. The district must give you, at your request, a list of places where you can obtain an evaluation. You might also check parent organizations, university special education departments, or even the telephone directory's yellow pages to locate appropriate evaluators. It is essential that the members of the independent evaluation team meet your state's certification requirements and that the assessment comply with evaluation requirements.

No matter who pays for it, the results of the independent evaluation must be taken into account by the district when it makes any decision about your child's educational program. You have a right to the reports of the independent evaluation team.

THE MANY DIMENSIONS OF EVALUATION

Because learning is such a complex process, and because so many factors affect school performance, assessing learning problems requires a multifaceted, multidisciplinary approach. The rest of this chapter describes the procedures most commonly used to evaluate a child who is thought to have a learning problem. It is extremely unlikely that your child will undergo all of these procedures, but the more extensive the learning problem, the more evaluation strategies are likely to be used. Figure 2.1 lists recommended areas of assessment for different disabling conditions.

Measuring Intelligence

Psychologists, philosophers, and educators have filled volumes with elaborate discourse on the meaning of intelligence, but have come no closer to consensus than they were centuries ago when the debate began. Perhaps the most valid conclusion to emerge from this debate is that intelligence has no fixed definition, since its meaning hinges on the context in which it is used. A definition that has gained wide but far from universal acceptance has been advanced by David Wechsler, whose 1974 manual to the *Wechsler Intelligence Scale for Children—Revised* defines intelligence as "the overall capacity of an individual to understand and cope with the world around him." From this perspective, intelligence

FIGURE 2.1 Evaluation Guidelines for Educational Disabilities

Exceptionality	Assessment data should be collected in the following areas:
Mentally retarded	Intellectual functioning, adaptive behavior, academic achievement, medical and developmental background, language usage
Hard of hearing/deaf	Audiological status, intellectual functioning, language usage, speech, academic achievement, social and emotional status, psychomotor ability
Speech impaired	Audiological status, articulation, fluency, voice quality, language usage, academic achievement, social and emotional status
Visually handicapped	Ophthalmological status, academic achievement, intellectual functioning, social and emotional status
Emotionally disturbed	Intellectual functioning, social and emotional status, adaptive behavior, academic achievement, medical and developmental background
Orthopedically impaired and other health impaired	Medical status, motor ability, adaptive behavior, intellectual functioning, academic achievement, social and emotional status
Deaf-Blind	Audiological status, ophthalmological status, language usage, medical status, adaptive behavior
Multiply handicapped	Medical status, intellectual functioning, motor ability, adaptive behavior, social and emotional status, academic achievement, language usage, speech, audiological and ophthalmological status (if appropriate)
Learning disabled	Intellectual functioning, academic achievement, language usage, social and emotional status, classroom behavior
Gifted	Intellectual functioning, academic achievement, social and emotional status, creativity

Source: Adapted from *A Primer on Individualized Education Programs for Exceptional Children* by Daniel P. Morgan. Copyright 1981 by The Foundation for Exceptional Children. Reprinted by permission.

might be viewed as a varied assortment of abilities allowing an individual to learn from experience, to solve problems effectively, and to adapt to changing environments.

How Smart Are Intelligence Tests? Given the differing views of what constitutes intelligence, it is not surprising that intelligence tests do not all measure the same mental abilities. As a result, you cannot meaningfully interpret results on a test of intelligence without knowing and understanding that particular test. Despite their different emphases, most intelligence tests assess a range of skills related to learning in school (as opposed to other kinds of learning). For this reason, most intelligence tests are global estimates of scholastic aptitude, that is, of a child's ability to succeed in school. Indeed, numerous studies have borne out the conclusion that IQ scores are relatively good, although far from perfect, predictors of later academic performance. Scores on an IQ test predict academic success about as well as a person's height predicts his or her weight.

On the other hand, intelligence tests do *not* measure innate potential to learn, nor do they assess a number of other factors associated with academic, social, and vocational success. They tell you nothing about your child's musical, artistic, or mechanical abilities; they provide only limited information on creativity, arguably a central component of intelligence; they suggest little about social skills or emotional maturity. It is therefore essential to supplement the measure of intelligence with an assessment of other skills.

In short, an intelligence test may predict your child's later academic performance, but it may also ignore many important facets of intelligence. Why, then, does it figure so often in an evaluation?

Why Measure Intelligence? A common but controversial tenet of psychological evaluation holds that intelligence testing assesses the student's overall capacity for academic growth. Assuming that intelligence tests are a valid yardstick of scholastic potential—and not all educators subscribe to this position—this information can, in conjunction with other data, help match your child with appropriate educational programs and approaches. Intelligence test findings also suggest the nature and extent of your child's learning problem. If despite conscientious efforts, Jeff falls substantially below grade level in academic performance, an assessment of his intellectual functioning may help determine whether his problem is related to a low level of intellectual ability (for example, retardation), or a learning disability, or emotional or motivational factors.

A case in point: a school psychologist was asked to evaluate Sharon, a fourth grader who was doing minimal academic work. She was described as "passive" and "slow" by her teachers, who thought she might be retarded. The psychological evaluation, which included an individual test of intelligence, showed that the teachers were wrong: Sharon was of "average" intellectual ability (she scored in the 65th percentile relative to other nine-year-olds). The psychologist looked at other aspects of Sharon's performance and concluded that her academic difficulties and passive behavior stemmed from her timidity, low self-esteem, and minimal self-confidence. She sat in the back row of a class of thirty-four children. Classroom observation suggested that when she did not understand something—as she often did not, due to her intense anxiety—she was afraid to question the teacher or even her classmates. Her teacher's rigid, intimidating style magnified this problem. Once these conclusions, and their instructional implications, were shared with the teacher, her work with Sharon changed. Sharon's seat was moved to the front of the class, where the teacher could monitor closely her grasp of the work. Also, the teacher encouraged Sharon to ask questions and to participate in situations where the teacher believed she would be successful. Sharon gradually showed signs of breaking out of her shell, although she remained somewhat shy and reticent; at the same time, her academic performance improved dramatically.

How Is Intelligence Measured?   Dozens of tests claim to measure intelligence. A test's quality hinges largely on the range of mental abilities that are assumed by the test developers to comprise intelligence, and the degree to which the test items reliably measure those abilities. A score on an intelligence test is therefore of little meaning without reference to the particular test used.

Some intelligence tests are administered to a group; others are administered on an individual basis. Group intelligence tests at best are useful screening devices, and should be interpreted with caution; they should not replace individual intelligence tests in the evaluation of students with learning problems.

Most individual tests of intelligence take forty-five to ninety minutes to administer. They should be given by psychologists trained in their administration and interpretation. They typically encompass a range of cognitive tasks of a verbal, conceptual, perceptual, and quantitative nature; most call for little or no reading. The test usually yields either an intelligence quotient (IQ), with 100 the "average" score, or a mental age, suggesting that your child's test performance is comparable to that of an "average" child of a particular age. The IQ test compares your child's performance with that of children of the same age who have taken the test. Many intelligence tests also have scale scores and subtest scores that allow for greater precision in the interpretation of results and identification of strengths and weaknesses.

Many people wonder about the stability of the IQ: how likely is it that a person's IQ will change over time? A number of research studies have shown that intelligence test performance tends to be stable over time with older students but relatively unstable with younger students; the IQ score of a six-year-old retested after. three years is more likely to change than that of a sixteen-year-old retested after a similar period. At the same time, numerous case studies of students of varying ages have documented marked, even drastic changes in IQ scores over time, in some cases as much as fifty points. These shifts frequently reflect dramatic changes in a child's life, for example, a change in the family structure or home situation. This underscores the importance of taking your child's environment and emotional status into account in interpreting the test results.

A Close-Up Look at an Intelligence Test. Despite the wide use of intelligence tests and their potentially dramatic impact, they remain mysterious to most laypersons. A fuller description of the individual intelligence test most frequently administered to children—the *Wechsler Intelligence Scale for Children—Revised* (WISC-R)—may shed light on what an intelligence test is and is not, and what skills it measures. The WISC-R tests the general intelligence of children age six through sixteen. The test consists of a Verbal Scale, which requires verbal responses to a range of tasks, and a Performance Scale, which generally elicits responses of a visual or visual-motor nature with minimal verbal content. Each scale contains six subtests that are described below.

THE VERBAL SCALE

1. *Information.* A child's fund of acquired information is assessed through such questions as, "How many months are in a year?" or "What is a thermometer?" Performance on this subtest reflects the range of the student's educational and environmental experiences.

2. *Similarities.* The evaluator mentions two items (for example, a pen and a typewriter) and asks what they have in common. This task requires the student to think abstractly or conceptually.

3. *Arithmetic.* The student responds orally to questions assessing

the ability to solve problems using a range of arithmetic operations. This subtest calls for focused concentration, short-term memory, and exposure to certain academic skills. It should not be viewed as a measure of the student's math achievement.

4. *Vocabulary.* The student is asked to provide definitions for a range of words. While this subtest is viewed as one of the WISC-R's more valid measures of intelligence, performance on this task is enhanced by an educationally "enriched" environment.

5. *Comprehension.* The student is asked a series of questions assessing familiarity with social customs and social practices (for example, "Why do people vote?"). These questions require logical thinking, social judgment, and what is ordinarily thought of as common sense.

6. *Digit Span.* The student is asked to repeat a progressively longer series of numbers, both forward and backward. This task, which is not considered in calculating the IQ score, requires close attention and short-term memory; performance is considerably affected by anxiety.

THE PERFORMANCE SCALE

1. *Picture Completion.* The student is shown a series of pictures and asked to identify a missing part in each. This requires attention to visual detail and the ability to distinguish essential from nonessential detail.

2. *Picture Arrangement.* The student is asked to arrange a series of pictures in a logical order to tell a story that makes sense. This task requires various skills, including an understanding of social situations, logical reasoning, and an ability to sequence in time.

3. *Block Design.* The student is asked to manipulate blocks to form a series of two-dimensional designs presented on cards. This abstract spatial-relations task requires the student first to analyze visually the design and then to synthesize or reproduce it.

4. *Object Assembly.* The student is asked to assemble puzzle pieces to form familiar objects. This tests ability to organize visually and to synthesize more than it tests motor skills.

5. *Coding.* This rote, timed task requires the student to reproduce on paper, as quickly as possible, newly learned material. Performance is enhanced by strengths in focused concentration, visual memory, and fine-motor agility.

6. *Mazes.* Using a pencil, the student proceeds through a series of mazes. This subtest, which is not used to calculate the IQ score, is rarely administered.

The student receives, for each of the subtests, a scaled score (which is different from the raw score) ranging from 1 to 19, with 10 the "average" score for children of that age. The verbal subtest scaled scores (excluding "Digit Span") are summed and the total score is converted into a Verbal IQ, with a norm of 100; the same process is carried out with the Performance Scale (excluding "Mazes") to obtain a Performance IQ. The scaled scores on the ten required subtests are added up and the total score is used to obtain the Full-Scale IQ, with 100 the norm. The WISC-R's standard deviation—a statistical property of tests—is 15, which means that approximately 68 percent of the general population will score between 85 and 115 on the test.

Scores are sometimes reported in terms of ranges and percentiles. For example, a psychological report might tell you that "Jennifer is currently performing within the 'high average' range of intellectual ability, equivalent to a percentile rank of 80 when compared to her same-age peers nationally." This means that on this particular test, Jennifer scored equal to or better than 80 percent of the students her age in the standardization sample. The WISC-R manual also provides these intelligence classifications which you may encounter in a psychological report:

IQ	CLASSIFICATION
130 and above	very superior
120–129	superior
110–119	high average
90–109	average
80–89	low average
70–79	borderline
69 and below	mentally deficient

When you look at the quantitative results obtained from an intelligence test, remember that it offers only a limited picture of your child's intellectual abilities. If no further information is offered, ask for more. It should be available, since the individual intelligence test can also provide the experienced, clinically oriented examiner with a wealth of information regarding your daughter's or son's cognitive strengths and weaknesses, thinking processes, approach to learning tasks, and emotional concerns. This information may suggest specific teaching strategies or modifications of the educational program appropriate to your child's learning style. Nonetheless, these conclusions should be confirmed, elaborated, or qualified using a range of other assessment procedures. Effective evaluators recognize the limitations of intelligence testing and take into account the potentially significant impact of environmental factors upon intelligence test performance. They know that such factors as cultural background, language problems, anxiety, inattention, and impulsiveness—to name only a few— can influence test performance. And they know that the results of these tests can sometimes prejudice our thinking. One Florida teacher reportedly gave his students more challenging assignments after he saw a roster with numbers from 130 to 150 after their names. He later found out that these were their locker numbers.

Finally, if you think that an evaluation relies solely or excessively on quantitative results of an intelligence test, you should discuss its scope with school officials; if you are still not satisfied, you might consider requesting an independent evaluation.

The Family Dimension

A comprehensive view of a learning problem requires an in-depth assessment of your child's history and home life. Your perspective is crucial to this part of the evaluation. Before we go any further, let's recall that here as elsewhere in this book, *parents* are defined as the adults who are most closely and consistently involved in the child's upbringing. In today's society, where a child's membership in a traditional nuclear family is not a foregone conclusion, these adults may or may not be the biological parents, but they nevertheless play an important role in the evaluation process.

A social and family assessment is typically conducted by a school social worker or a school psychologist who meets with you—one or both parents—either at school or at home. (If the parents do not live together, *home* means where your child usually lives.) Ideally, all the adults directly involved in your child's upbringing should be present. If both parents are in the household, it is important to obtain both perspectives to understand fully the family dimension of the learning problem; in divorced families, both parents' perspectives are still valuable. If your household consists of, say, a parent and a grandparent, or a parent and a step-parent, it is a good idea for both to take part in the interview. It may even be useful to include your child (and brothers or sisters) so that the evaluator gets as much useful information as possible, and several perspectives on relevant family interactions.

What will the evaluator want to know? That depends on the professional's training and theoretical approach, as well as on your child's age and the identified problem. Most likely, questions will be asked in these areas:

- family status, past and present;
- your child's health, past and present;
- your child's developmental history;
- your child's educational history;
- your child's current status;
- your perspective on your child's problem.

The information gleaned from this meeting often proves crucial in understanding the dynamics of your child's learning difficulty, and evolving ways to help school staff, your family, and your child cope with the problem. A thorough assessment will probably point to contributing factors. While some, such as birth complications, do not admit change, others do, and the evaluator may discuss with you ways that you can help your child at home. The meeting also gives you a chance to ask questions and express your concerns to a professional who is experienced in working with students with disabilities and their families.

Will the questions be embarrassing? Probably not. The discussion may touch on sensitive issues, but it must always be geared in some way to understanding and alleviating your child's possible learning problems. If you don't see how a particular question relates to your child's education, ask for an explanation before you answer the question. (An interviewer cannot collect information just for the sake of completeness or just to have general background data.) If you are not satisfied with the explanation, you are free not to answer.

A word about your family's right to privacy. First, you can refuse to have school officials visit your home and instead opt for a meeting at school. The bottom line is: use your good judgment, and keep in mind that the interviewer is bound by law to respect your privacy. Any information that you provide can be divulged legally only to school staff who will be working with your child; no information can be released to persons outside the school without your written consent. Exceptions to this are noted in the discussion of school records, later in this chapter.

The Social and Emotional Dimension

Emotional concerns and conflicts can dramatically affect classroom performance. You know all too well how an argument at home, a family member's illness, even the death of a pet—not to mention such traumas as a divorce or the death of someone close—can disrupt your child's concentration. Emotional distress can also affect the learning process in more subtle ways, contributing to a child's difficulty in mastering a particular skill. Some child psychologists have taken the extreme position that many reading problems stem from underlying emotional issues. Bruno Bettelheim advances this view in *On Learning to Read*.

At the same time, it is widely recognized that learning problems, and the frequent accompaniments of frustration and discouragement, can give rise to emotional difficulties, which may further hamper the child's ability to learn. This vicious circle of frustration and failure is all too often the learning-disabled student's strongest association with school. As a result, self-esteem and self-confidence typically take a dive.

How can you tell if this is happening to your child? A conversation with the classroom teacher may help. Some children are lively at home but withdraw from the learning process, becoming passive and sullen in class and taking little part in class or social activities; others seek attention and recognition from teachers and classmates by becoming the class clown or picking fights or defying the teacher. Or, a learning-disabled youngster may refuse to surrender to this discouragement, demonstrating resilience and perseverance despite steep barriers to learning.

Your child's social and emotional experience is a central component of any school-based psychological evaluation. The school psychologist gathers information from a range of sources to understand whether, and how, these concerns are affecting school performance. In addition to consulting with the teacher and other school staff, obtaining information about your child's family life, and reviewing the school file, the school psychologist may also assess your child's social and emotional status through classroom observation, a clinical interview, and formal testing.

Classroom observation is important: by visiting the classroom even for twenty minutes, a psychologist can often find out a great deal about your child's style of interactions, level of self-confidence, and mood. The "clinical interview" may sound more dramatic than it is:

the school psychologist has a chat with your child. This is not psychotherapy: here again, only information crucial to educational decisions should be gathered, and your child's privacy must be respected.

The school psychologist may give your child a range of tests, including projective tests, sentence-completion tests, rating scales, and self-report measures to gain insight into your child's thoughts, feelings, and social capabilities. Projective tests present relatively ambiguous, unstructured questions or tasks, which have no right or wrong answers, allowing a child to give answers that "project" aspects of his or her personality. The results permit a psychologist to draw inferences about your child's emotional needs and concerns. The projective test may be as simple as asking a child to draw a picture of a person and then tell a story about the drawing. The psychologist develops hypotheses about the child's self-concept based on the content of the drawing (but not its artistic value) and the accompanying story. For instance, your child's perceptions of family dynamics—of how he or she fits into the family constellation—may be gleaned from drawings of the entire family. Another frequently used projective technique, picture-story assessment, asks a child to look at pictures and then invent stories based on them. The psychologist assumes that the themes emerging in the stories represent important issues in your child's emotional life.

The psychologist may also make use of adaptive behavior measures to assess your child's level of personal independence and social competence. These measures—which psychologists are using with increasing frequency—take the form of questionnaires completed by you or your child's teachers (or anyone else who knows your youngster well) to get a relatively objective measure of his or her adaptive behavior relative to other children of the same age. These tests are particularly valuable with children who are thought to be mentally retarded. Indeed, the evaluation and classification of a child as mentally retarded requires an assessment of adaptive behavior.

The Academic Dimension

School staff or you may initiate an evaluation if your child is thought to have an educational disability. One essential question the evaluation should answer is: does your youngster indeed have a problem in learning? An educational evaluation determines the current level of academic skills, takes stock of specific strengths and weaknesses, and explores problem areas by detecting error patterns. This evaluation will probably furnish information that serves several purposes. Most basically, it gauges your youngster's level of achievement in reading, mathematics, and written expression. These levels are not always evident from classroom performance; indeed, many children are thought, on the basis of class work, to function below grade level until individual tests of academic achievement demonstrate their mastery of grade-level skills. Such a discrepancy indicates that other factors, such as low motivation or poor work habits, may be hampering classroom performance. Or, the child may happen to be in a class of predominantly high achievers where average grade-level performance based on national standards falls below the group's standard.

Achievement tests establish skill levels in various areas, and can be critical in suggesting a learning disability, as in the case of a hard-working student whose academic skills fall significantly below grade level. But these tests are of limited utility if they only indicate the grade levels of your child's academic skills; they should also provide information on specific academic skill mastery and on the child's way of approaching academic tasks. Knowing that your seventh-grade daughter is reading at the 4.1 grade level won't help the school very much in developing an educational program without concrete information about her specific strengths and weaknesses.

An educational evaluation therefore has a broader scope, assessing your child's mastery of academic skills, his or her approach to learning tasks, external factors influencing academic achievement, and the instructional strategies that address individual needs. It encompasses not only formal and informal testing, but also observation, review of the educational history, and consultation with classroom teachers. The assessment tasks vary according to your youngster's age and learning problem; for example, the evaluation of your six-year-old includes more perceptual, fine-motor, and gross-motor tasks than that of your fourteen-year-old.

A premise that has long dominated the field of special education is that learning problems, particularly in reading, result from deficits in perceptual or perceptual-motor development. This process-oriented approach assumes that progress in academic skills such as reading hinges on the development of basic perceptual skills. This theory holds that if the perceptual "apparatus" is not functioning effectively, information from the environment is not conveyed to the brain accurately, or the person's thoughts are not expressed correctly, resulting in interference with the learning process.

As a result of these assumptions, tests assessing perceptual and perceptual-motor skills are a routine part of educational evaluations. Research, however, has not supported the underlying premise that these skills are necessary for normal academic achievement, and thus throws into doubt the use of some of these tests for diagnosing learning disabilities. While future research may suggest a more useful role for these tests, particularly in the auditory modality, their current utility in the evaluation of children with learning disabilities is limited. A more useful approach appears to be the assessment and remediation of the learning task itself. For example, when a child is experiencing reading difficulties, it is important to analyze performance in the component skills of reading (for example, the ability to use word parts such as prefixes, suffixes, and root words) and then develop teaching strategies that specifically address these weak areas.

The educational assessment may be conducted by a number of different professionals in the area of special education depending on what state you live in. In some states, this is the job of a learning specialist, who may be called a learning consultant or an educational diagnostician; in other states, it may be the job of a school psychologist.

OTHER ASSESSMENTS

While psychological and educational assessments are the most typical means of evaluating your child, evaluators may want to look at other dimensions of the learning problem as well. Some of the other common assessments are discussed below.

Medical Examination

Every child with a suspected educational disability should undergo a thorough medical examination, preferably by a pediatrician. A doctor may pick up physical problems that interfere with your child's ability to learn in school. For example, a child who appears inattentive in school and has difficulty understanding directions may suffer from allergies; a youngster who is lethargic in class may have anemia, hypoglycemia, or glandular problems; a child who appears to daydream frequently may actually suffer from petit mal seizures. Accurate diagnosis of these or other problems not only assures proper medical treatment, but also suggests alternative ways of responding to your child in school. While the school will likely offer to arrange a medical examination by its own physician, you usually have the option of submitting the results of a recent examination by your child's doctor.

Neurological Examination

Since the brain is the primary organ associated with learning, your child may benefit from evaluation by a neurologist—a physician who specializes in the functioning of the brain and the central nervous system. It is preferable, though not essential, that the doctor be a pediatric neurologist.

Aside from an examination, the neurologist may rely on other sources of information, including the family history, developmental and medical history, observation of the child, and reports of functioning at home and in school. Typically, the neurological assessment includes a general physical examination that takes into account a range of mental, sensory, and motor abilities that are directly affected by the functioning of the brain and the central nervous system. The neurologist may ask your child to perform a variety of unusual (but typically unthreatening) tasks, for example, touching the right hand to the left ear, putting marbles in a cylinder, or naming the body parts. Based on these and other procedures, the neurologist makes a judgment about the relative normality of your youngster's neurological status.

Another diagnostic tool sometimes used by the neurologist is the electroencephalogram (EEG), a painless procedure that measures the child's brain waves. It does *not* measure intelligence. The EEG was initially thought to have great promise as a diagnostic tool with the learning-disabled, but it has proved of limited value except in the detection of seizure disorders. While research shows that children who have learning disabilities are, as a group, more likely than other children to have abnormal EEG readings, it is also true that some 15 to 20 percent of *all* children—including normal achievers—have abnormal readings. In short, the EEG results are an unreliable indicator of a learning disability; however, advances in computer analysis of the EEG offer some promise in assessing people with learning disabilities. For the time being, the EEG should be included in the evaluation only if the neurologist suspects that your child may have a seizure disorder or if appropriate computer analysis services are available.

Don't be alarmed if the evaluation of your child includes a neurological examination. Only in rare cases does such an examination detect a specific neurological syndrome such as a seizure disorder or a brain tumor. Much more often, neurologists find "soft signs"—ambiguous evidence suggesting a neurological problem. These soft signs might include problems in such areas as speech articulation, coordination and balance, memory, imitating motor movements, and fine-motor movements. While children with learning disabilities often manifest some of these soft signs, their occurrence does not necessarily indicate the presence of a neurological problem or brain injury.

Nevertheless, many specialists have assumed that clusters of these symptoms indicate what has been called "minimal brain dysfunction" (MBD). Use of this term has been criticized for three good reasons: it is ambiguous; it groups together children with very different characteristics into a disease category; and it has little utility in suggesting a treatment or educational approach. Despite these problems with terminology, it is widely recognized that a significant proportion of children with brain injuries do have learning disabilities.

In summary, a neurological examination contributes to the overall evaluation of your child's learning problem when the focus is on determining his or her general neurological development relative to other children of the same age; identifying or ruling out specific problems of the central nervous system; and suggesting appropriate medical treatment or educational intervention for a possible disorder.

Psychiatric Examination

Children with learning difficulties often exhibit behavioral or emotional problems in school. These problems sometimes reflect discouragement and low self-esteem, stemming from frustration and failure in school. If the school psychologist thinks that serious emotional problems are hindering learning, he or she may recommend an assessment by a psychiatrist—a physician specializing in the diagnosis and treatment of emotional disturbance. (In some states, only on the basis of a psychiatric examination can a student be classified as "emotionally handicapped" or "emotionally disturbed.") Like the psychological assessment, this assessment seeks insight into the factors contributing to these problems, and possible interventions. The nature of the psychiatric assessment varies substantially with the particular psychiatrist, the nature of the problem, and the child's age. The psychiatrist may want to speak with you and will be particularly interested in knowing whether your child is receiving any medication for school-related problems (for example, for "hyperactivity") and, if so, whether you have noticed any reactions.

Vision Examination

If your child is experiencing learning problems, it is a good idea to find out from the start whether information is being properly received through the senses. Your youngster probably has already gone through the vision screening that most schools administer in the early grades, but these tests often provide limited information. Many of these school vision tests, such as the standard *Snellen Wall Chart*, only assess central visual acuity. If your child has a possible vision problem, he or she should be seen by an ophthalmologist—a physician specializing in the treatment of eye disease—or an optometrist—a nonmedical doctor specializing in diagnosing and correcting impaired vision. Many people have the misconception that children with learning disabilities often have vision problems. In fact, the suspicion of a learning disability does not automatically indicate the need for a detailed vision examination. The American Academy of Ophthalmology has issued a statement asserting that learning-disabled children are no more prone to vision problems than normally achieving children. In particular, the tendency to "reverse" letters in reading is not usually caused by a vision problem.

Hearing Examination

Approximately 3 percent of school children have a hearing impairment. Because imperfect hearing can seriously hamper a child's learning, you should lose no time in looking into a possible problem. You and other family members are in the best position to detect a hearing loss, but teachers may also observe its signs. (See Appendix A.) As part of its overall evaluation, the school district will most likely conduct a hearing test; group tests are considerably less valid and reliable than individual hearing tests which use, for example, a pure-tone audiometer. If a more in-depth audiological (hearing) evaluation is warranted, your youngster will likely be referred to an audiologist or to a physician specializing in ear problems (either an otologist or otolaryngologist).

Speech and Language Assessment

Because a child who experiences learning difficulties is particularly prone to communication problems, the evaluation may include a speech and language assessment. These problems may range from difficulty in producing specific speech sounds to a total inability to use speech and language to communicate. A speech therapist (who may also be called a speech correctionist, speech clinician, or speech and language pathologist) may assess a number of areas, including speech articulation, speech fluency, voice characteristics, and expressive and receptive language skills.

This assessment can provide significant insights into a child's inability to grasp basic academic skills, and may suggest the need for speech or language therapy as well as specific strategies for remediation in the classroom.

Occupational Therapy Assessment

If the evaluation suggests that your child has difficulties with fine-motor or gross-motor movement (as many children with learning problems do), an occupational therapist may be called in to assess the child's ability to integrate different mental and motor processes in a purposeful manner. The assumption underlying this evaluation is that many tasks required of children in and out of school are complex actions involving a chain of more basic processes; a breakdown in one of these processes can interfere with the child's success in the more complex task. The seemingly simple act of copying a word from the blackboard, for example, requires a child to use appropriate pressure on the pencil, hold the paper with the other hand, determine where to begin writing, accurately perceive the symbols and break them into their component parts, and reproduce the letters on paper using, among other things, proper eye tracking. If the writing task, or other school-related tasks which require motor or perceptual-motor skills, pose problems, the occupational therapist evaluates a wide range of motor and visual-motor actions to determine if there is any breakdown in the underlying processes, and if necessary develops an appropriate program of remediation. Another important focus of occupational therapy, when appropriate, is self-care or personal independence skills (for example, grooming, dressing, and feeding).

Physical Therapy Assessment

Occupational therapy is distinct from but complementary to physical therapy, which is used with children who have primarily lower extremity gross-motor problems. If your child has physical limitations, the school district may conduct a physical therapy assessment, and may recommend physical therapy to improve gross-motor skills and increase the strength and endurance of body parts. Physical therapy may be recommended, for example, if your youngster has a neuro-muscular disorder such as cerebral palsy or muscular dystrophy, or a muscle-skeletal disability such as spina bifida; it may also be recommended to help your child with a less debilitating physical disability.

SCHOOL RECORDS

The evaluation process yields a wealth of information about each student. Much of this information is recorded in writing and placed in individual student files. It may be placed in a "cumulative file"; this is a file kept on all students in the school they attend and contains such items as health information, past and present grades, standardized test scores, and anecdotal reports from teachers. More likely, it will be placed in a "confidential file"; this is a file kept for each special education student either in the school of attendance or in a centralized district location and contains such items as the referral form, individual evaluation reports, the Individualized Education Program, and correspondence between the school district and parents.

You may have concerns about how records on your youngster are kept and used, since they may contain sensitive or personal data about your child's life at home and at school, and because the information—test results, classification, psychologists' reports, etc.—can potentially shape perceptions and affect your youngster's later opportunities. You have reason to take care that these files be kept confidential and that they not be misused. In the past, there has been abuse: records have been kept from parents' eyes but shared with too many other people. Such abuses may still occur, but today they are illegal. Legal safeguards are provided by the *Family Educational Rights and Privacy Act of 1974* (which you may know as the Buckley Amendment) and Public Law 94–142.

LEGAL SAFEGUARDS ABOUT STUDENT RECORDS

• *Parents' Access to Records.* Parents—and students if they are over age eighteen—are entitled to examine all "education records" that the school district maintains, in any location. (A natural parent without custody of his or her child has access to these records unless a legally binding document states otherwise.) What are "education records"? The Buckley Amendment defines them as *any* records kept by the school district directly related to your child. An exception is made for information collected and recorded but not shared with any other person (such as personal notes jotted down by a psychologist during an evaluation). You are, of course, not entitled to review records on other children.

You can request to review your child's records by writing a letter to or phoning the principal (for a cumulative file) or director of special education or special services (for a confidential file). District policy may require a written request. The school district must comply with your request for review of your child's records within forty-five days of the request and prior to an IEP meeting or a due-process hearing. You are also entitled to have any other person of your choosing review the records (such as other family members, an outside educator, a psychologist, doctor, or lawyer). It is a good idea to examine the evaluation reports before the IEP meeting so you can participate as fully as possible.

• *Explanation of Records.* The school district must respond to your reasonable request for explanations and interpretations of the records. You may ask a school official to review them with you, or you may prefer to review the records in private. Federal law does not require the presence of a school representative when you review the records.

• *Release of Records.* Your written consent is required before your child's records can be released to anyone (with limited exceptions, such as school employees with a "legitimate educational interest" in the information, state and federal education officials, officials of a school district in which your child is planning to enroll, and court officials). Prospective employers therefore cannot receive information from your child's school records without your consent. How do you know who has seen the files? The school district must maintain a record of persons who have examined or received information from a child's records (except parents and authorized school employees). You are permitted to review this record. If you move to another school district, you may review the records and request information you want sent to the new district.

• *Requests for Copies.* You can request copies of your child's records. The school district may charge you a reasonable fee for making them, unless the fee precludes your having access to the information. You may also take notes from the records.

• *Amendment of Records.* If you believe that information contained in the records is inaccurate, misleading, or unnecessarily invasive of your child's or family's privacy, you may request that the records be amended by either adding or deleting information. Make this request in writing to the principal or director of special education or special services. The school district must respond to this request within a reasonable period. If the district refuses this request and the dispute cannot be resolved informally, you can initiate a hearing.

• *The Hearing.* The provisions for a hearing to resolve a dispute about education records are described in the Buckley Amendment. (This hearing is different from the impartial due-process hearing detailed in Public Law 94–142.) The hearing can be conducted by any party—including a school official—who has no investment in the outcome of the dispute. You can present evidence and be represented by an attorney. The rules for this type of hearing are quite straightforward, but like any legal proceeding, it can get more complicated in practice. If the hearing officer decides that the information is inappropriate, the record must be amended accordingly. Even if the information is found to be appropriate, you have the right to insert into the record a statement commenting on the disputed information or indicating the reasons for your disagreement. This statement must remain in the record as long as the contested information is kept, and must accompany the contested portion whenever it is released to any party.

• *Destruction of Information.* The school district must notify you when information in the record is no longer directly relevant to the education of your child (for example, when he or she graduates or is no longer eligible for special education). The information must be destroyed at your request. Before you order any information destroyed, however, remember that certain information may be needed for noneducational purposes (such as documenting entitlement to social security benefits).

• *Student Access to Records.* When your youngster reaches age eighteen, he or she gains the rights regarding education records discussed in this section.

FOR FURTHER INFORMATION

The Family Educational Rights and Privacy Act Office, U.S. Department of Education, Washington, D.C. 20202, is a federal agency that can answer your questions and investigate your complaints regarding any aspect of school records.

Bettelheim, B., and Zelan, K. (1982). *On learning to read: The child's fascination with meaning.* New York: Knopf.

Boehm, A.E., and White, M.A. (1982). *The parents' handbook on school testing.* New York: Teachers College Press. An excellent, example-filled guide to the types of tests used in schools. Discusses how to make sense of the results and what questions parents should ask.

Buros, O.K., ed. (1978). *Eighth mental measurements yearbook.* Highland Park, N.J.: Gryphon Press. An encyclopedia of psychological and educational tests that provides up-to-date reviews of most published evaluation measures. May be available in your local public library.

Children's Defense Fund (1981). *Your school records.* Washington, D.C. A booklet that reviews your rights regarding your child's school records, relevant legislation, ways of effectively gaining access to records and preserving their confidentiality, and steps that you can take when you are in conflict with the school regarding educational records. [See Appendix B]

Dyer, H.S. (1980). *Parents can understand testing.* Columbia, Md.: National Committee for Citizens in Education. A 92-page booklet that provides an overview of school testing programs and examines issues of educational evaluation, including minimum competency testing. [See Appendix B]

Klein, S.D. (1978). *Psychological testing of children—A consumer's guide.* Boston: Psy-Ed. A 41-page compact guide that effectively demystifies the testing process. Written in jargon-free, readable prose.

Wodrich, D.L. (1984). *Children's psychological testing—A guide for nonpsychologists.* Baltimore: Paul H. Brookes. This 180-page book makes accessible to laypersons the basic principles of child development and psychological measurement. It reviews more than fifty tests, from infant scales to preschool and school-age tests.

3

The Individualized Education Program: Legal and Procedural Issues

A basic premise of special education is that the instructional program must be carefully tailored to an individual's learning characteristics and educational needs. Special education instruction has not always been individualized, however. Indeed, in the past students with very different educational needs were often given identical educational programs. Fortunately, these and other inappropriate educational practices are now less common. Today it is not only an accepted premise but also a legal mandate that your youngster's special education program be designed to meet his or her specific needs. The formal mechanism for accomplishing this, the Individualized Education Program (which you may know as the IEP) is the subject of two chapters. This chapter takes a look at the legal and procedural issues involved in the IEP process; the next chapter discusses the wide range of alternatives and considerations involved in developing the IEP.

THE IEP: CORNERSTONE OF SPECIAL EDUCATION

Public Law 94–142 requires the development of an IEP for *every* student who qualifies for and receives any special education services through the public schools. The IEP spells out an intensive program of individualized instruction designed to help eliminate or compensate for the obstacles to learning stemming from your child's disability. As the primary vehicle for ensuring the provision of a free appropriate public school experience for students with educational disabilities, the IEP is at the heart of Public Law 94–142. The IEP is *individualized* in that it is based on your child's educational needs rather than on those of a group; its focus is *education* (although this is interpreted liberally in relation to the instructional needs of students who have disabilities); and it is a *program* in that it constitutes an explicit description of the services which must be provided.

The IEP is both product and process. The product is the written document detailing the special education program. The process entails not only the design of the program, but also its implementation and the monitoring that ensures it is put into effect as planned. By law, the IEP designed for your child must be developed by a team of people directly involved with him or her, including the teacher and including you. In this way, the process brings together at a single meeting the individuals who best know your child's educational needs so that they can share information and arrive at a plan of action that takes into account various perspectives.

WHAT MUST THE IEP CONTAIN?

A comprehensive plan of action—in education as in any other field—defines where you are now, where you are heading, how you intend to get there, how long it will take, and how you can be sure that you've arrived. Accordingly, Public Law 94–142 states that the IEP designed for your child must contain six essential ingredients; it must spell out the following:

- your child's level of educational performance;
- annual goals and interim, short-term objectives;
- special education and related services that will help your youngster to meet these goals and objectives;
- the extent to which your child will participate in the regular education program with children who do not have educational disabilities;
- projected start-up dates for services and their expected duration; and
- objective criteria, evaluation procedures, and a schedule for assessing, at least once a year, your youngster's achievement of the goals and objectives.

When you attend the meeting at which the document is drawn up—the IEP meeting—keep in mind that the IEP must include all special education and related services required to meet your child's educational needs without regard to what services the school district has available, the cost of those services, any inconvenience to administrators posed by those services, or the adequacy of the current staff to provide them. For instance, if the IEP team determines, on the basis of an evaluation, that your youngster needs speech and language therapy, school officials cannot legally refuse this service on grounds such as these: "We don't have a speech therapist at this school," or "Our speech teacher can't travel across town just to see one student." If the IEP states that your child, who uses a wheelchair, requires transportation home after orchestra rehearsals, the school district must comply.

The bottom line is that the school district must implement the IEP as written. If the school system cannot meet your child's needs in a program within the district, it must obtain the services from another public school system or from a private agency, and it must foot the bill. A district cannot simply place a student on a waiting list for a special education program or a related service (although the law does allow for some reasonable delays in carrying out the program).

The IEP covers *all* areas or subjects in which your child receives special education, even if that specialized instruction takes place in a regular education setting. For some students, the IEP is restricted to one or two academic areas. A youngster with a physical disability may require special education—and therefore an IEP—in physical education only; a child who has a speech impairment may have an IEP that covers only speech articulation; an IEP for a student who has a more severe disability or multiple disabilities would probably encompass a greater portion of the overall instructional program.

The IEP is a comprehensive blueprint for special education, but it is not a daily lesson plan. It does not—and should not—detail the teaching objectives and strategies for each day's instruction. While the daily instructional objectives derive from and are consistent with the IEP, the teacher needs flexibility to adjust the day's activities in accordance with your youngster's progress.

WHO DEVELOPS THE IEP?

The IEP process assumes that each key person involved in the education of your child has a role to play in designing the program. The framers of Public Law 94-142 mandated that, at a minimum, a school official, the classroom teacher, a parent, and possibly the child meet to draw up an IEP. (This is the group we have called the IEP team, although it goes by different names in different states.)

A school official. A school staff member (other than the classroom teacher) who is qualified to supervise the special education program and who has the authority to commit the resources necessary to implement the program must attend the IEP meeting. The individual may be a special education administrator, a principal, or a member of the evaluation team such as a school psychologist; this varies with the school district and with the nature and severity of the learning problem. If your child has been evaluated for the first time, a member of the evaluation team (or someone else who is knowledgeable about the evaluation results) must be present.

The classroom teacher. The observations of your child's classroom teacher are crucial to program decisions that are appropriate and can be put into practice effectively. Also, the teacher who has actively participated in developing an instructional plan is more likely to be committed to seeing it through. For these reasons, it is important that school officials do whatever is necessary (such as authorizing sufficient released time) to enable the classroom teacher to take part in drawing up the IEP.

You, the parent. Like most parents, you may not have the expertise to make decisions regarding teaching approaches or curricular materials, but you can contribute to the IEP process your extensive knowledge of your child's style of learning and his or her strengths and weaknesses. The role envisioned for you by the framers of federal special education legislation is not that of a passive recipient of information, but rather an active participant. When possible, all of the adults who are directly responsible for your child's day-to-day upbringing are encouraged to attend. (This may mean mother and father, or another combination of parenting adults.) Chapter 5 suggests strategies for your involvement in the IEP process.

Your child, when appropriate. Your child may be capable of participating meaningfully in the developing of the IEP. Many youngsters are—particularly older students. All too often, they have been excluded from taking part, even though their input and reactions might be very helpful as the IEP team considers the appropriateness of different placement options, defines goals and objectives, and considers possible obstacles to the program's success. If your child is present, the IEP meeting provides an opportunity for you and school staff to explain the evaluation results and the rationale for the planned program. The school should raise the option of including your child at the meeting before it takes place; if school officials don't mention the possibility, don't hesitate to raise the subject yourself. Remember that you have some flexibility here. For instance, you may decide with school officials that your child should only attend part of the meeting.

Other persons. You can invite other persons to attend the meeting, as can the school district. While a small group is best—you obviously don't want to call a town meeting—you may wish to invite a guest who can provide vital information or expertise or simply serve as an objective observer. You might want to bring another parent more experienced in the IEP process, or a friend, relative, or advocate. A previous teacher or tutor might have ideas or observations to offer. Depending on the issues that are likely to come up, you might want to consider inviting a legal adviser, private evaluator, family doctor, or a therapist. The school may request the attendance of an administrator, one or more members of the evaluation team, a guidance counselor, additional teachers, a physician, or a school nurse.

WHAT IS THE TIME FRAME?

The IEP must be completed and implemented with minimal delay. The regulations accompanying Public Law 94–142, described below, are quite specific, and state regulations often impose further time restrictions.

- A meeting to develop the IEP must be held within thirty calendar days of the determination of special education eligibility.
- The special education program must be implemented as soon as possible after the IEP is completed, although reasonable delays are allowed for such circumstances as school holidays or special transportation arrangements.
- The IEP must be completed *before* the program starts, whether your child begins the program in September or during the school year.
- The entire IEP must be reviewed at least once each year for every student to determine if it remains appropriate, and if not, to revise it.

YOUR PARTICIPATION

To make it possible for you to take part in the IEP meeting, the school district must

- give you adequate notice of the meeting;
- let you know the time and location of the meeting (which should

be agreeable to you), its purpose, and the names of all participants;
- inform you that you may invite other people, including your
  child, to the meeting;
- make available an interpreter to you if you have a hearing impairment, or if English is not your first language, so that you can
  understand and participate in the discussion.

How you are notified is left up to the school district: they may phone
you, send a letter, arrange an informal conference, or make a home
visit.

If, despite diligent efforts by school staff, you cannot attend the
meeting or choose not to, the school district must try to find other
ways to involve you in the IEP process, including individual or conference telephone calls. An IEP meeting may be held without you only
after the school has made vigorous efforts to get you to attend. But
even if the IEP meeting is held without you, your consent remains
necessary before your child can be placed in a special education program for the first time.

THE IEP MEETING

Ideally, the meeting is a gathering of equals, each with a unique
perspective, at which program decisions are made by consensus.
School staff (for example, the evaluation team) may meet without you
before the IEP meeting to integrate evaluation results, discuss your
child's eligibility for special education, and go over possible program
options and tentative goals and objectives, but by law the actual IEP
can be developed and made final only at the IEP meeting, with all the
required participants in attendance, and not before. Nor is the IEP to
be developed by any one person; the law intends it to be a shared effort reflecting diverse perspectives. You must be given a chance to
contribute to all aspects of the IEP before it is completed.

The name and format of the meeting may vary with the district.
Some districts ask you to attend two meetings: one to review the findings of the evaluation team and to discuss your child's eligibility for
special education, and another to draw up the IEP. Other districts inform you of the evaluation results and eligibility status in a letter and
then hold a meeting to develop the IEP. Still other districts put all these
tasks on the agenda of a single meeting.

The responsibility of the IEP team, at a minimum, is to arrive at a consensus about the components of the IEP so that the program meets the standards of "appropriateness" and "the least restrictive environment" as well as the other legal requirements. Other issues may also be discussed and decided upon, including the concrete steps of program implementation, plans for home-school communication during the school year, and arrangements for follow-up meetings.

If the IEP is developed as envisioned in the law, the meeting takes a minimum of one hour (and probably longer if the program is complex). If the meeting is adjourned after ten or fifteen minutes, this might be a signal to you that something in the IEP process is amiss, and that the program being developed for your child may not comply with legal standards.

The meeting may go very smoothly: you and school staff may be on the same wavelength. Or, you may disagree with some aspect of the proposed program. If this occurs, school officials are required to let you know about the due-process procedures available to resolve disputes. Chapter 7 has much more to say about conflict-resolution procedures.

THE IEP DOCUMENT

As long as the IEP includes the six required elements, federal regulations do not require that it take a specific form. As a result, there are myriad forms in use throughout the country. Some are short, while others are long and complex. A typical IEP runs about three to five pages. The most useful IEP documents are written in plain, understandable language and are relatively free of educational jargon. While there is no standard form used nationwide, figure 4.1 (in chapter 4) shows you what a typical goals and objectives section might look like.

The IEP is considered an "education record" and is therefore subject to the same confidentiality safeguards as any other school record, in accordance with the *Family Educational Rights and Privacy Act*. It cannot be released to anyone outside the school district without your written consent (with a few rare exceptions). The school does not need your consent, however, to share the IEP with school staff who are directly involved with your child or who have a valid educational interest in the information. The completed IEP must be given to you at your request; many districts provide you with a copy as a matter of policy.

LEGAL STATUS OF THE IEP

While the IEP is not a legal contract, the school district is required by law to provide all the services described in it for the specified time period. At the same time, school districts are under no obligation to provide special education services that are not described in the IEP. These principles underscore the document's importance. If the school district fails to provide the educational services spelled out in the IEP or changes the special education program without an appropriate IEP review meeting (which you attend), you can challenge the school's actions through due-process procedures.

The IEP sets forth goals and objectives for your daughter or son, and the school district must provide the services specified in the document to help your youngster reach those milestones; but federal regulations explicitly state that the school district and its staff are not legally bound to ensure that your child actually attains the goals and objectives. In short, the district cannot guarantee success. The thinking behind this principle is that the learning process is subject to too many factors beyond the control of school officials to obligate the district to a specified level of student performance. School districts are, however, required to make a good-faith effort to help your child achieve the goals and objectives and, if they are not met, must review the program's suitability and revise it as necessary.

YOUR CONSENT

Your written consent is required before a school district can place your child for the first time in a special education program. (Figure 5.2 is a checklist that helps you decide whether the IEP is appropriate and whether you should consent to the program it describes.) Before requesting your consent, the district must inform you in writing of the rationale for the program. This statement may be incorporated into the IEP or may constitute a separate document. While the law does not require that the IEP itself be signed, many districts request you to sign it to signify your consent to the program. Other IEP team members may sign it as well to document their participation in the meeting. Your consent is considered valid when

- you have been given all pertinent information;
- you understand and agree in writing to the educational program; and

- you are aware that consent is voluntary and can be withdrawn at any time.

If you do not consent to the initial special education program, the school district cannot implement the program unless it obtains a decision in its favor from an impartial hearing officer at a due-process hearing. Even then, you still have the right to appeal this decision to a higher authority, as does the school district if it does not prevail at the hearing.

Your consent is not required for any changes in the special education program once the initial program is in place. However, you are not powerless if you disagree with the school's recommendation. The school district must notify you in advance of the change and must invite you to a new IEP meeting to revise the IEP. The special education program cannot be changed without such a meeting. While your consent is not required at this point, due-process procedures are still available to you if you take issue with school officials' decisions or actions. If you notify the school in writing of your intention to challenge the recommended program change (see chapter 7), your child remains in the present program until resolution of the dispute. In practice, school districts are often reluctant to change a child's special education program without parental approval, and will try to resolve the conflict in a manner suitable to both parties without recourse to a due-process hearing. This underscores the importance of making your views known to school officials.

4

Developing the IEP

The special education program flows directly from the decisions made at the IEP meeting and, more specifically, from the contents of the IEP document. Since the school district must provide the services described in the IEP, it is crucial that the document be comprehensive and precise. This chapter takes a close look at each of the required elements of the IEP and discusses the range of program alternatives available for special education students.

CURRENT EDUCATIONAL STATUS

This section of the IEP describes your child's present level of educational performance, focusing on strengths as well as weaknesses. It takes stock of the skills your youngster has and has not mastered. This kind of inventory is an essential step in translating the evaluation results into a practical instructional plan. It can be most useful when it

   draws from a variety of information sources;
   explains the effect of the disability on academic and nonacademic
      areas;
   identifies concrete and specific skills and behaviors and mini-
      mizes global statements;
   avoids the use of labels or jargon;
   portrays *current* skills; and
   explains the implications of test scores.

The description of your child's current educational status will vary with the nature and severity of the learning problem. For a student with a speech impairment, this section may be narrow in scope; for a youngster with multiple disabilities, it will probably encompass several academic and nonacademic areas.

GOALS AND OBJECTIVES

On the basis of the current educational status, the IEP team develops annual goals and short-term objectives. An annual goal sets out what your child is realistically expected to accomplish in a particular area in one year. Each goal is broken down into short-term objectives, each specifying a step that your child is expected to make toward the annual goal in a shorter time, such as a marking period; objectives are milestones which mark progress between your child's current skill level and the annual goal. Goals and objectives provide direction to you and the teacher and facilitate the evaluation of your youngster's progress and program.

The IEP team is required to write goals and objectives only for the areas in which your child qualifies for special education, that is, those in which he or she cannot substantially benefit from the regular education materials and methods. Consider a wide range of instructional areas; your child may need specialized instruction not only in reading and math, but also in such other areas as self-care skills, fine-motor and gross-motor skills, social skills, and vocational education, to name only a few. (In the areas in which your child does not need special education, he or she is expected to follow the regular education curriculum and objectives.) Thus, the number of goals and objectives will likely increase with the severity of the disability and with the scope of the special education instruction. Once the areas requiring special education have been identified, how does the IEP team go about formulating goals and objectives? It can use such sources as scope-and-sequence charts, criterion-skill checklists, and curriculum guides to identify appropriate goals and objectives, or it can develop them on its own. A commercially available curriculum guide, which lists instructional objectives in sequential order, is the *Objective Cluster Banks* series, published by Edmark Associates, P.O. Box 3903, Bellevue, Wash. 98009 (1-800-426-0856).

Goals should be written first, since they get broken down into the more specific statements called objectives. While goals and objectives differ in terms of time frame and degree of specificity, they consist of the same three elements.

- *The desired behavior or skill.* Use terms that are specific, observable, and, when possible, measurable to describe what you expect your child to accomplish. Avoid terms that are subjective and open to interpretation (for example, "to enhance self-concept").

- *The conditions under which the behavior is to occur.* Be specific in stating when and/or where the behavior is to occur (for example, "during gym" or "by the end of the first marking period").
- *The desired level of performance.* This allows you, school staff, or your child to determine whether the goal or objective has been achieved. The criterion should be observable and, when feasible, expressed in quantitative form (for example, "Complete 85 percent of all math assignments" or "Attend school 95 percent of the days").

While more general than objectives, goals should nonetheless be specific enough to provide direction to the teacher. The following are examples of goals that might be found in an IEP.

Clarence will attend school 170 of 180 possible school days.

Rebecca will write from memory the letters of the alphabet in the upper and lower cases without error.

Jennifer will achieve a reading grade-level score of 3.5 in the area of word-attack skills on the *Woodcock Reading Mastery Tests* when tested on May 30.

Lisa will achieve at the 6.5 grade level in math by June 1, as measured by the *Key Math* test.

Wendy will improve her ability to multiply and divide with decimals, as evidenced by her performance in the resource room.

Michael will correctly tell the time to the minute using the classroom wall clock.

Allan will improve his ability to play in group games on the playground without peer conflict.

Each goal should be composed of at least two short-term objectives, which are to be arranged in a logical sequence for instructional purposes. The following are some examples of short-term objectives:

Given a list of twenty words, Kevin will be able to place them in alphabetical order with 100 percent accuracy.

Billy will state orally five words that illustrate the final "e" principle.

Given a list of twenty three- and four-syllable words, Judy will correctly indicate the syllables in at least sixteen.

Jose will correctly subtract a two-digit number from another two-digit number without regrouping in eighteen of twenty problems.

Debbie will read chapters 1 and 2 of *America's Story* (Book I) and achieve a score of at least 80 percent on each of the chapter tests.

Shannon will hand in 90 percent of her math assignments during the first marking period.

James will maintain eye contact with the teacher or other students for a minimum of ten seconds in at least 75 percent of his "show and tell" presentations.

David will stuff envelopes with the address showing in the envelope "window" with 95 percent accuracy.

Figure 4.1 provides an example of a completed goals and objectives section of an IEP for one instructional area.

Writing goals and objectives can be an arduous, time-consuming process, but it is important not to lose sight of their ultimate intent: to guide the teacher in working with your child and to help determine whether your child is progressing in the specified areas. If goals and objectives are written with this in mind, the time invested by you and school staff is likely to yield high educational dividends.

SPECIAL EDUCATION PLACEMENT

The IEP must specify the special education and related services needed to meet the identified goals and objectives—without regard to the educational programs the district has available. It must also indicate the degree to which your child will participate in the regular education program. This latter requirement may be fulfilled by indicating the percentage of time in a regular education program or by listing the regular classes and activities your son or daughter will attend.

The special education placement—that is, the type of educational setting in which your child receives the specially designed instruction—is at the heart of the IEP. It largely determines the intensity of the specialized instruction your youngster will receive and the extent of his or her contact with students who do not have educational disabilities. Indeed, the majority of the disputes between schools and parents of special education students focus on the placement.

FIGURE 4.1 Sample Sheet from an IEP

Instructional Area: Academic Readiness

Current Level of Performance: At present, Eric recognizes the upper-case letters B, C, E, H, I and L. He does not recognize any lower-case letters that assume a different form from the corresponding upper-case letters. He can print his name in the upper case; but is not yet able to print any other letters.

Annual Goal: Eric will recognize and write all the letters of the alphabet in both the upper and lower cases.

Short-term Instructional Objectives (including criteria for success)	Instructional Methods and Materials	Person Responsible for Implementation	Evaluation Procedures	Date of Review
1. When presented visually with each of the letters of the alphabet (both upper and lower-case), Eric will state the name of each with 100% accuracy on two separate occasions.	• V.A.K.T. Approach • Sandpaper Letters (J.A. Preston Corp.) • Alphabet Cards (Developmental Learning Materials) • Visual Readiness Skills – Level 1 (Continental Press)	Resource Room Teacher	Informal assessment through presentation of alphabet cards	10/15/86
2. When presented orally with each of the letters of the alphabet, Eric will print all the letters (both upper- and lower-case) with 100% accuracy on three separate occasions.	• [Same as Above] • Tracing Paper Designs (Developmental Learning Materials)	Resource Room Teacher	Informal assessment through oral presentation of letters	1/15/87

Determining an Appropriate Placement

The IEP team identifies a special education placement that meets the student's educational needs as embodied in the goals and objectives. Federal law requires only that it be an "appropriate" placement rather than "the most appropriate" placement, as many believe. The placement must be derived from careful assessment of these educational needs, rather than directly from the student's disability or classification. If Nancy has been classified as "emotionally handicapped," for example, she should not be placed in a special education class for the "emotionally handicapped" simply by virtue of the classification. She might be able to perform satisfactorily in a regular classroom with support from a school psychologist, with modifications made by the classroom teacher, and with some instruction in a resource room program. Nor should a student who is severely disabled automatically be placed in a special school. Many blind students can be successfully educated in a regular school and, in some cases, in a regular class with supplementary aids or services.

What is an "appropriate" educational program? This question has sparked frequent disagreements between parents and schools. The U.S. Supreme Court had an opportunity to clarify the meaning of "appropriate" in 1982 in the case of *Board of Education* v. *Rowley*, when it ruled that a hearing-impaired child is *not* entitled to a sign-language interpreter at public expense to help her achieve her full potential. In so doing, the Supreme Court established a principle that applies nationwide: an "appropriate" education is one that will "permit the handicapped child to *benefit educationally* from the instruction" (emphasis added). The good news is: federal law obliges your school district to provide services to help your child profit from instruction; the bad news is: federal law does *not* oblige school districts to help your child reach his or her full potential.

Another issue that has been the subject of litigation is the length of the school year. Special educators have long known that over the summer months, some children with disabilities experience a significant loss of skills—or a "regression," as educators may say. Are these children entitled to year-round services? Courts have generally ruled that children with special needs, particularly those with severe disabilities, can be considered for educational programs that extend beyond the 180-day school year to ensure maintenance of their skills. Deciding which students qualify for an extended school year (sometimes abbreviated ESY) has presented states with a difficult problem, and has resulted in differing interpretations of the legal mandate. What is clear is that the decision is to be based on the educational needs of an individual student. If you believe that your child's academic skills will weaken markedly over the summer and that extended educational services are therefore needed to prevent this skill loss, present your views at the next IEP meeting, or request a new meeting before the scheduled date.

Legal Requirements

Public Law 94–142 sets forth regulations that govern the determination of a special education placement. These are summarized below.

- The special education placement decision is to be made by a team of persons, including you, who are knowledgeable about your child, the evaluation results, and the special education process.
- The special education placement is derived from a range of sources, including tests, teacher recommendations, and your child's physical, cultural, and social characteristics, and is based on the IEP.
- You must provide written consent before your child can be placed for the first time in a special education program.
- The school district must provide a continuum of special education placements to meet the needs of students who have educational disabilities.
- Your youngster can only be removed from the regular education program when he or she is not able to receive an appropriate education in the regular education program, even with the use of supplementary services.
- Your child must be educated with nondisabled students to the maximum extent possible.
- Your child must be placed in the school he or she would attend if not disabled unless the IEP indicates otherwise.
- The placement is to be made as near to the student's home as possible.
- In making the placement decision, the IEP team should consider a placement's potentially harmful impact on your child or on the quality of the program.
- The special education placement must be reviewed at least once per year.

- You must be notified a reasonable time before the school district proposes to change the placement of your child.

Placement Alternatives

School districts must make available a range of educational placements for students with disabilities. This legal mandate recognizes that these students have diverse educational needs, and that only a variety of educational settings can meet the needs of all students with disabilities.

School districts may fulfill this mandate by providing programs within the district (for example, a resource room in a regular school) as well as outside the local district (for example, regional, county, or state programs, or private schools). Your child's placement, whatever the setting, is without cost to you. Special education placements range from programs offered in the child's regular school to special schools, home instruction, and hospitalization.

Regular Class with In-Class Accommodations. Your child may be able to learn effectively in a regular classroom if the teacher modifies the instruction or the curricular materials, and uses specialized equipment when necessary (for example, a braille typewriter). Can your youngster's needs be met entirely in the regular class? This depends on his or her learning profile relative to those of classmates, the teacher's skills, the teacher-student ratio, and the available resources. To be successful, this arrangement usually requires the ongoing consultative assistance of a specialist such as a special education teacher or a school psychologist.

Regular Class with Supplemental Services. With this type of placement, your child remains in the regular class for most of the day but also receives specialized instruction from another school staff member outside the regular classroom. This most often takes place in a ''resource room,'' where students receive intensive small-group instruction from a teacher certified in the education of the handicapped for a portion of the day. The amount of time and the focus of instruction are based on your child's individual needs and must conform to the IEP. The resource room teacher uses specialized teaching approaches and employs materials and equipment typically not available to a regular classroom teacher. State laws contain more specific resource-room regulations (for example, the maximum amount of time a student can spend in a resource room, or the maximum number of students a resource-room teacher can instruct at any one time). Another kind of supplemental program is provided by a school staff member such as a speech and language therapist or occupational therapist who provides "related services." These services are discussed later in the chapter. No matter what form the supplemental program takes, coordination with the regular classroom instruction is crucial.

Part-time Special Education Class (Regular School). If the IEP team determines that your child's educational needs cannot adequately be met in a regular class, even with accommodation by the regular teacher or supplemental services, placement in a special education class is the likely outcome. A special education class is an educational setting for a relatively small group (approximately five to sixteen students) of youngsters with educational disabilities who typically spend most of the school day in that class. It is taught by a teacher certified in the education of the handicapped and may have the benefit of one or more teaching aides.

States vary in the restrictions placed on special education classes. In many states, they are organized according to the state's classification system so that students recommended for special education classes must be placed in the class appropriate to their classification; for example, an "emotionally handicapped" student recommended for a special education class would be placed in a class for "emotionally handicapped" students. In other states—New York, for example—special education classes are organized according to the severity of the student's learning problem and not according to the student's classification. Whatever system is used to organize special education classes, the intent is to group together students with comparable educational needs and similar physical and social development. States may also place restrictions on the maximum number of students in each type of special education class and the age range of the students in the class.

A student may attend a special education class for a portion of the school day and participate in the regular education program for the remainder of the day. The student may be placed in regular classes (that is, mainstreamed) in nonacademic subjects (for example, physical education, music, or art) or academic subjects in which the student can learn effectively.

Full-time Special Education Class (Regular School). A student who is unable to perform adequately in any mainstream subject, either academic or nonacademic, may be placed in a special education class for the entire school day in a regular school. This kind of placement should be rare, since appropriate mainstreaming opportunities can usually be found for most students.

Special Education Class (Special School). If your child's learning problems are so extensive that his or her educational needs cannot be met in a regular public school, the placement may be a public or private school restricted to students with special needs. Such a school can orient its programs, policies, staff, and resources to meet the needs of students with learning problems. Some special schools provide programs for students with a range of disabilities; others such as a school for the deaf are for students who have a specific disability. Some special schools may arrange for their students to be mainstreamed when appropriate and feasible in nearby regular schools.

Home Instruction. Your child may be provided with instruction at home by a certified teacher if the school is in the process of arranging a special education placement or if your youngster is unable to attend school temporarily for medical reasons.

Hospitalization or Residential Placement. If your child's medical or psychological problems are severe enough to warrant a more restrictive setting, he or she may (with your consent, of course) be hospitalized or placed in a public or private residential program in which academic instruction is usually available. In addition to receiving an educational program, your child would, in such a placement, receive treatment for the problem that justified the placement in the first place. A primary goal of hospitalization or residential placement should be to facilitate your child's return at the earliest possible time to a less restrictive setting. Who arranges for this kind of placement, and who pays for it? In many cases a state agency does both. Or, if the state is unwilling, you have the option of making private arrangements and footing the bill (or obtaining insurance coverage). In either case the local school district may pay the cost of your child's educational program.

Placements Outside the Local School District

School districts must give priority to placing students who have disabilities in *local* educational programs. If appropriate programs are not locally available, school districts may arrange an educational program in a public or private school outside the local district. Public Law 94–142 includes regulations governing these out-of-district placements. Here is a summary of the more significant of these regulations:

- Placement by a local school district in an out-of-district school is without cost to you.

- The local school district must develop an IEP for your child before it places her or him in an out-of-district school.
- The local public school district must prepare and implement an IEP to guide the special education services it provides, even if these services are provided in a private school.
- The local school district is ultimately responsible for the special education programs it provides for your child even if it makes an out-of-district placement, unless responsibility for your youngster's education has been explicitly assigned to a state agency. The district therefore assumes responsibility for ensuring that there is an appropriate IEP, that the special education and related services described in the IEP are provided, and that the IEP is reviewed at least annually.
- If your child is placed out of the district for special education services, a local school district representative must nevertheless participate with you in all meetings to develop or revise the IEP.
- If your child is placed in an out-of-district school, he or she has the same rights and is entitled to the same safeguards as special education students served within the district.
- If you choose to send your child to a private school despite the availability of an appropriate special education program within the public school system, the school district is not obliged to pay for the tuition. However, according to a 1985 U.S. Supreme Court decision, if a court or state agency determines that your placement of your child in a private school was necessary to obtain an appropriate education, you are entitled to reimbursement for tuition.
- Students in public or private institutions cannot be denied access to an education in a regular public school if it is an appropriate placement.

The Least Restrictive Environment

The principle of the "least restrictive environment" mandates that students with special needs participate in as much of the regular education program as is appropriate to their educational requirements. In other words, your child should not be isolated from students without disabilities any more than is educationally necessary. The assumption underlying this principle can be stated simply: the education of disabled students with nondisabled students is beneficial to both groups and is therefore to be encouraged as much as possible. This interaction can enhance the self-esteem, confidence, and social skills of students with special needs and promote understanding and acceptance by students without special needs.

In implementing the least restrictive environment mandate, the task of the IEP team is to identify the educational placement that (1) can meet the needs of your child and (2) approximates as nearly as possible the educational experience your child would receive if he or she did not have an educational disability. To do this, the team members consider a range of placement alternatives according to the degree to which each deviates from the regular education program. Figure 4.2 depicts the special education placement alternatives along such a continuum.

The lowest step of the pyramid is the special education placement most closely resembling the regular education program. As you move up the pyramid, the program becomes more removed from the regular education program and provides less involvement with nondisabled students. The IEP team's job is to choose the lowest step on the pyramid that meets your child's educational needs. If your youngster is already in a special education program, the IEP team must review the IEP to see whether your child is ready to take a step down the pyramid to a less restrictive educational setting (or, if necessary, move up the pyramid). The review process ensures that your child's placement does not become an educational dead end.

The determination of the least restrictive environment is based on your child's learning and behavioral characteristics. The least restrictive environment for Yvonne will not necessarily be the least restrictive environment for Brandon, even though both have the same classification (mildly retarded) and both are seventh graders. Placement in a regular class with supplemental instruction in a resource room might be the least restrictive setting for Yvonne, while Brandon might require a special education class to learn effectively. The IEP team thus engages in a balancing test in which it weighs the academic and social advantages and disadvantages of different potential settings. In any case, the least restrictive environment principle is *not* a mandate simply to place students with disabilities in regular classes, as it has sometimes been interpreted.

The following examples illustrate how this least restrictive environment concept works in practice.

1. Sean is a second grader classified as "emotionally handicapped" whose reading skills are at the mid-third grade level and

FIGURE 4.2 The Placement Pyramid

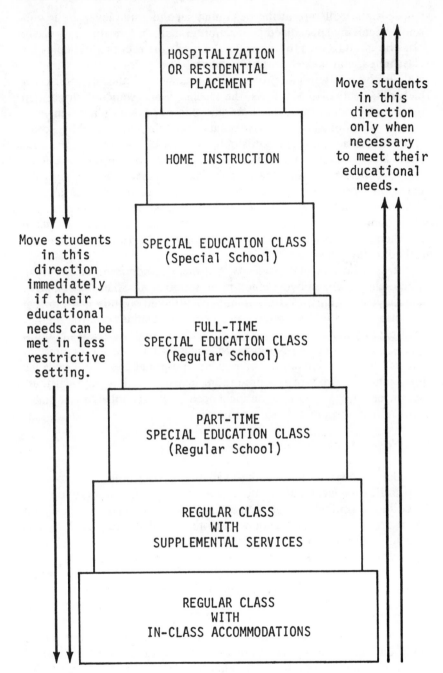

whose math skills are at the beginning second-grade level; he is currently receiving specialized instruction in math in a resource room. In class he often refuses to follow the teacher's instructions, ridicules his classmates, and makes disruptive noises during classroom lessons; in addition he is often inattentive to the lessons and almost never completes his seatwork. Mr. Ross, the teacher, understandably frustrated by the way Sean drains his time and energy, favors placement in a special education class. The IEP team cannot simply accept Mr. Ross's recommendation, however; it is obliged to make sure that a concerted effort has been made to resolve Sean's problem at the regular education level before deciding that this setting is no longer appropriate. So, the team works with the school psychologist to develop an explicit behavior management program that Mr. Ross can implement in the classroom. If this and other efforts prove unsuccessful, the IEP team can then consider a more restrictive educational setting such as a special education class.

2. Sharon is a first grader with a medical condition called spina bifida, characterized by a defect in the spinal cord. Sharon's cognitive and academic skills are only minimally affected by this neurological condition, but she does have a problem with bladder control. Rather than placing her in a special education class, the IEP team—mindful of the least restrictive environment mandate—develops a program that allows Sharon to remain in her regular first-grade class: she receives forty minutes a day of resource-room instruction, has physical therapy twice a week, and has continual access to a school aide who takes her to the bathroom at frequent intervals.

The Nonacademic School Program

School districts must make available to your child the same opportunities to participate in nonacademic subjects and activities offered to the general school population. This legal mandate is designed to ensure that special education students are not shortchanged in their educational experiences because of their disability. These nonacademic activities must be provided with nondisabled students to the greatest extent possible. Your child must therefore have the opportunity to be in a regular homeroom and to take such subjects as art, music, home economics, industrial arts, and vocational education. Physical education in particular is intended to be an integral part of the educational program for children with special needs. It must be adapted, if necessary, for your child's participation (often called "adaptive physical education"). Other nonacademic subjects must also be modified within reason if necessary for your youngster to benefit from the instruction. Of course, any significant modifications should be noted in the IEP.

The school district must also provide opportunities for your child to participate in any extracurricular activities available to students who do not have disabilities, including class trips, assemblies, hot lunches, student committees, sports programs, clubs, musical groups, safety patrol, health services, and employment services. If, for instance, a physically disabled youngster's ninth-grade class is visiting a museum, your daughter cannot be excluded because the bus won't accommodate her wheelchair. The school must provide special transportation to get her there. Nor should a student be automatically excluded from such school areas as the playground, cafeteria, snack bar, regular school bus, library, or study hall because of a disability. (Court rulings have helped define the obligations of local school districts in providing nonacademic services for students.)

Selecting a Placement

Federal law specifies legal requirements to which the special education placement must adhere, but it provides little guidance in selecting a placement. You can help to decide whether there is a good match between your child's needs and the proposed placement, and can help to predict its likelihood of success. Since few placements will meet *all* of the criteria described below, you and other members of the IEP team must decide which are most essential to your child's well-being. You may ask a number of relevant questions.

- *How many students are currently in this special education placement?* The teacher-student ratio will affect the intensity of the individualized instruction your youngster will receive.
- *Are my child's academic skill levels comparable to those of other special education children with whom he or she will be grouped?* While a special education teacher is trained to provide individualized instruction to all the students in the class, a wide discrepancy in students' skill levels makes this more difficult.
- *Is my child compatible with the other students in the placement?* Peer relationships in the special education placement are likely to affect your child's motivation, work habits, behavior, and confidence. If peer incompatibility seems likely (for example, if your daughter is placed in a class with students two to three years younger than she, or if your emotionally and physically fragile son

is placed in a class of streetwise, "tough" youngsters), it is important to take steps to prevent a problem from occurring and to be prepared to handle a problem if it does occur.

• *Will the placement have any harmful effect on my child?* According to Public Law 94–142, the IEP team must consider the potentially negative impact of the placement on your child (for example, a severe loss of self-esteem).

• *Will my child disrupt or impede the education of other students if placed in a regular class?* Section 504 of the Rehabilitation Act of 1973 explicitly states that placement of a child with special needs in a regular class is not appropriate if the student is disrupting classmates' education.

• *Is the teacher's instructional style compatible with my child's educational needs?* Teachers' instructional styles can be structured or unstructured, firm or lenient, formal or informal, serious or humorous. Some teachers are more effective with an angry aggressive youngster; others work better with the alienated, unmotivated student; still other teachers are effective with the shy, insecure student. Similarly, different students respond to different teaching styles. Your son or daughter may learn most effectively with a teacher who sets firm limits, or one who is sympathetic and nurturing, or one who rigidly structures classroom tasks. You might also consider whether the teacher has training and expertise in an academic approach needed by your child; whether your youngster responds better to a male or female teacher; or whether your youngster seems to do best with one or a number of teachers.

• *What resources will be available to my child in this school?* Your child's learning program may suggest the need for specialized teaching materials or equipment. Special education placements differ in terms of access to these resources.

• *Does one or more aides assist the teacher in this placement?* Some states may mandate the presence of an aide to assist the teacher for certain special education placements. School districts may provide aides even if they are not legally required to do so. The presence of an aide generally allows for closer monitoring of your youngster's academic performance.

• *What is the school's general climate with regard to students who have disabilities?* Each school has its own distinctive personality, which is often a reflection of the leadership and initiatives of the principal. While a cross-section of attitudes can always be found among staff members, many schools can be characterized according to their receptivity to the education of students who have disabilities. Some schools are very willing to make accommodations that benefit special education students; other schools are more resistant to modifying educational programs. Try to determine whether the school actively promotes interaction between students in regular education and those in special education.

• *Where is the school located?* Federal law clearly states that (1) preference should be given to the school your child would attend if there were no disability; and (2) your youngster should attend school as close to home as possible. These regulations aim to provide your child with a placement that resembles as closely as possible the program he or she would receive if there were no disability. They also seek to avoid a long bus ride; some states have imposed limits on the length of bus rides.

• *Are the school's important facilities physically accessible to my child?* Federal law (Section 504) obliges school districts to make their schools accessible to students with disabilities. This may be accomplished through such modifications as building ramps, installing handrails, redesigning equipment (for example, placing a desk on blocks to accommodate a student in a wheelchair), or relocating classrooms. Structural modifications are only necessary when less costly changes cannot provide access. While the school need not be entirely free of architectural barriers, it must be sufficiently accessible to students with physical disabilities so that they can attend the school and participate in its activities.

• *Where is my child's classroom located within the building?* The location should minimize its special status. Locating a special education class in a separate wing, a trailer, or a basement where no regular classes meet inappropriately draws attention to the special status of the placement, and needlessly isolates your child. Another consideration is the classroom itself: is it conducive to learning? Special education classrooms in your district may be required to meet state regulations regarding space, ventilation, noise level, and number of children.

• *What opportunities are available for mainstreaming my youngster?* A student placed in a regular school will likely have the opportunity to be mainstreamed in the full range of regular education subjects and activities. Special education schools, however, vary in the ease with which they can mainstream students for part of the day. Some have arrangements with nearby public schools so that mainstreaming can take place with minimal inconvenience and interruption of the program.

• *What is my child's reaction to the placement? What is my overall reaction?* Your child's acceptance of the special education placement and your support are critical to its success.

• *What opportunities are available for parent participation?* While most special education teachers will welcome your involvement, the nature of this participation will vary with each teacher. Inquire about such issues as the frequency and format of parent contact, opportunities to visit the class and serve as a classroom aide, and behavior modification programs coordinated between home and school.

MAINSTREAMING

The IEP team's primary focus is to develop an individualized program of special education. While federal law requires that the IEP team describe only the amount of time your child is in a mainstream program, it is nonetheless important that the team—and you, as part of the IEP team—carefully plan for your youngster's mainstream program to enhance its likelihood of success.

Mainstreaming is the provision of appropriate instruction for students who have disabilities in educational settings with the general student population. Mainstreaming is *not* the automatic placement of students who have disabilities in regular education settings. The least restrictive environment mandate of Public Law 94–142 requires that students with special needs be placed in as much of the regular education setting as is appropriate to their educational needs. Implicit in the practice of mainstreaming is the assumption that students with and without disabilities are more alike than different and that, with adequate training and support, regular educators can provide appropriate instruction to students with a range of skill levels.

The first step is to decide whether your youngster is ready to be mainstreamed, and if so in what areas. There is no simple formula or battery of tests to assess your youngster's readiness for mainstreaming. Rather, the decision requires careful consideration of your child's learning characteristics as well as those of the educational setting. In short, the IEP team must determine not only whether the student is ready to be mainstreamed but also whether the school is prepared to mainstream the student. The mainstreaming decision must be based on the school's ability to provide instruction that will benefit the student in a regular education program; it is not necessarily based on the severity of the disability.

When you and school staff evaluate whether—and in what areas—to mainstream your child, you might consider:

- your youngster's desire to be mainstreamed;
- your youngster's skill levels in the area or subject under consideration;
- the minimum skills needed to benefit from the regular class instruction;
- the kind of educational program and approaches to which your child responds best;
- the organizational structure and academic demands of the mainstream class (for example, note taking, textbooks, homework, tests, and grading);
- the number of students in the class;
- the presence of other children with special needs in the class (often it is desirable to have more than one child who has a disability in a mainstream class);
- the attitude of the mainstream teacher toward teaching children with special needs;
- the mainstream teacher's skill, experience, and degree of success in teaching students with similar educational disabilities;
- the availability to the mainstream teacher of any special materials and equipment needed to teach your child;
- the support available to the mainstream teacher from other school staff;
- the likelihood that your child will be accepted and supported by classmates and the opportunities for positive social interaction;
- the academic and emotional support that your family is able to give your child to reinforce the efforts of the mainstream teacher.

You can have a voice in both shaping the mainstream program and monitoring its effectiveness. By talking with your child, reviewing schoolwork, and keeping in touch with the classroom teacher, you can assess whether your child is understanding and keeping up with the assigned work and whether any problems are impeding performance. You will need to differentiate between mild initial adjustment problems in the mainstream class that are to be expected, and more serious problems that are likely to continue and may require a program adjustment or change. Keep in mind the mainstream program's primary purpose in assessing its effectiveness; for example, placement of your daughter or son in a social studies class may be primarily intended to provide opportunities for social interaction with a varied group of classmates in an academic setting.

RELATED SERVICES

Your child may receive *related services* to reinforce the special education program. The related service may allow your son or daughter to be placed in a less restrictive educational setting than if it were not provided (for example, providing in-school counseling to a student with emotional problems). Related services are typically provided by a specialist outside the classroom individually or in small groups. This specialist may also consult with your child's classroom teacher in order to coordinate the related service with classroom activities.

Public Law 94–142 lists and defines the following related services for which your child may qualify:

audiology services
counseling services
early identification
diagnostic medical services
occupational therapy
physical therapy
psychological services
recreation
school health services
social work services
speech pathology
transportation

The federal regulations also list counseling and training for parents as related services. You may qualify for such a program in your district. This listing does not exhaust the related services that your daughter or son might receive. Other related services may be provided by an interpreter for the hearing-impaired, or a reader and mobility specialist for the visually impaired. You can obtain further information about the nature and purpose of related services by writing to associations specific to that service, some of which are listed in Appendix B.

One particular related service—transportation specially arranged for students with disabilities—can give rise to problems and require careful planning. Your child may ride the regular bus or walk to school; or, your child may require special transportation if there is no regular bus route (for example, if your youngster attends a special education class in another district) or if special arrangements (such as the assistance of an aide or special equipment on the bus) are needed.

Procedural Issues

How do you know if your son or daughter qualifies for related services? Federal regulations set forth specific procedures concerning these services. They are highlighted below.

- Decisions about which, if any, related services your child will receive, and how much or how often, are made by the IEP team at the IEP meeting. These decisions are based on the results of the various evaluations and, if necessary, the recommendations of a specialist in the particular area.
- Your daughter or son is eligible for a related service when the IEP team determines that the related service is, in the words of Public Law 94–142, "required to assist a handicapped child to benefit from special education." Your child may be eligible for a range of related services, or may qualify for none. Once his or her eligibility is established, the IEP team should determine and state on the IEP the frequency of the service and, when appropriate, the length of the sessions.
- The related service described in the IEP must be provided by the school district in the amount specified without cost to you. Once the IEP team decides that your child qualifies for a related service, it cannot legally be withheld because it is unavailable in the district. If necessary, the district must obtain and pay for the services from agencies or individuals outside the district.
- The nature or amount of the related service cannot be modified without holding another IEP meeting; telephone contact is acceptable where parents are unwilling or unable to attend. The service can be discontinued if the original problem is no longer present (for example, if a speech-articulation program is corrected) or where you and the school agree that it is no longer appropriate.

EVALUATION OF THE IEP

How will you know whether the IEP goals and objectives have been attained? One section of the IEP itself is devoted to this question. It gives you and the school specific procedures and criteria for evaluating the IEP, and in this way provides a barometer of your child's progress and the program's effectiveness. The program evaluation results may also indicate that the educational services need rethinking or that the goals and objectives are unrealistic and need revision.

The evaluation process may be incorporated into the goals and objectives section or may be a separate part of the IEP. Whatever the format, the IEP evaluation process should be directly linked to the goals and objectives and should include a description of the procedures to be used in assessing the program's effectiveness; the evaluation criteria, namely, the expected levels of performance for the goals and objectives; and a statement as to when the program evaluation will take place.

WHEN DO SERVICES START? HOW LONG DO THEY LAST?

By law, the IEP must specify when the special education and related services will begin and how long they are to continue. This helps to ensure that the program will be implemented in a timely way and will not be discontinued prematurely. Public Law 94–142 requires that the IEP be implemented "as soon as possible" after the IEP meeting, with exceptions allowed if transportation needs to be arranged or if the IEP meeting is held during a vacation period. Some states impose a maximum number of days following the IEP meeting within which the IEP must be put into effect. If the delay is minimal, the program change might wait until after an event that is important to your child (for example, an eagerly anticipated holiday party or class trip) or until after a short schedule break (for example, after the end of a marking period or a vacation). The special education placement will usually continue for a minimum of a year, or at least through the end of the school year, at which time the program will likely be reviewed and revised if necessary.

ADDITIONAL IEP ITEMS

The IEP components described above represent the minimum requirements as mandated by Public Law 94–142. Some states have gone beyond these federal standards by requiring that other items be included in the IEP: for example, New Jersey requires the writing of an instructional guide, which details methods and materials to be used with the special education student. The IEP team may, of course, include other relevant information in the IEP beyond that required by federal or state regulations. Here are examples of additional items that you may ask to have included in the IEP:

- significant dates (for example, dates of referral, evaluations, eligibility determination, and IEP development);
- IEP team members;
- persons who will implement educational services in IEP;
- specialized teaching materials and equipment;
- specific teaching strategies compatible with your child's learning style;
- regular education subjects and programs in which your child will participate;
- strategies for social and emotional development;
- alternative disciplinary measures;
- your child's daily (or weekly) schedule;
- extracurricular activities;
- alternative classroom testing procedures (for example, use of oral exams in place of written exams);
- district testing status (indicating whether your youngster is required to take district-wide standardized tests, possibly with modifications);
- graduation requirements (see chapter 6);
- your child's native language (if other than English); and
- suggested activities that you can do with your child to reinforce the special education program.

REVIEW OF THE IEP

The requirement that the IEP be reviewed annually, or more often if necessary, aims to ensure that the program continues to be appropriate and remains the least restrictive educational setting. The IEP review meeting, which must include a school district representative, your child's teacher, you—and, if you wish, your child—can take place at any time during the year; it is often held at the end of the school year or on the anniversary date of the last IEP meeting. This review meeting supplements (but does not take the place of) established school procedures for informing you of your child's progress (for example, report cards or parent-teacher conferences).

The IEP is not carved in stone. The IEP describes a full year's program, but this does not preclude the IEP team from revising the IEP during the year. You or the school can request a review of the IEP prior to its scheduled date. You can request an early review through a letter to the principal or the district's director of special education or special services. The school district must honor any request for an IEP meeting that you make.

The participants in the IEP review meeting—including you—examine your youngster's school performance by considering reports by the teacher and other school staff, test results, your child's own observations and reactions, grades, work samples and whatever feedback you can offer.

Here are questions that should be on your mind as you sit at the review meeting:

- Has the IEP been implemented as written?
- Has my child been receptive to the instruction?
- What obstacles, if any, have gotten in the way of my child's academic or social adjustment?
- To what degree has my child attained the goals and objectives in the IEP?
- Does my child continue to need special education instruction? If so, in what areas? What goals and objectives should be pursued?
- What is now the appropriate, least restrictive special education placement? When will it begin?
- Has my child made progress in the areas in which he or she is receiving related services? Are they still needed, and, if so, to what degree?
- Does my youngster's performance during the past year indicate the need for alternative instructional strategies or additional specialized materials or equipment?
- How will the new program be monitored? When will the new IEP be reviewed?
- What questions, concerns, and reactions do I have about my child's special education program? Can I get any further suggestions about how I can support my child's educational program?
- What significant changes, if any, have taken place in our family, or in my child's health, that might affect academic performance?

By discussing these and other questions, the IEP team arrives at a revised IEP which will be in effect for the following year, or until the next review meeting. Remember that you retain the same legal safeguards at the review meeting as you had at the initial IEP meeting, including the right to challenge any decision through the applicable due-process procedures.

FOR FURTHER INFORMATION

Arena, J. (1978). *How to write an I.E.P.* Novato, Calif.: Academic Therapy Publications. This guide provides a good introduction to the IEP process in less than 100 pages, and discusses practical considerations in developing the educational program.

Morgan, D. P. (1981). *A primer on individualized education programs for exceptional children.* Reston, Va.: Foundation for Exceptional Children. This 120-page book examines the issues involved in developing an IEP in a way that recognizes the complexity of the process and potential obstacles to its success. Provides useful lists, figures, and sample IEPs, and makes frequent reference to research.

Nazzaaro, J. (1979). *Preparing for the I.E.P. meeting: A workshop for parents.* Rosslyn, Va.: Council for Exceptional Children. A multimedia kit (including a guide, filmstrip, and audiocassette) designed for use with groups of parents.

Turnbull, A., Strickland, B., and Brantley, J. (1982). *Developing and implementing individualized education programs.* 2d ed. Columbus, Ohio: Charles E. Merrill. This 384-page book leaves few stones unturned in discussing the IEP process. The extensive appendix provides a wealth of information, including checklists of school-related behaviors, sample IEP formats, and curriculum checklists.

5

Parents as Partners
in the Special Education Process

When you think back to your school days, you probably remember that your parents were only called into school if you were having a problem. Most likely they went with trepidation and sat quietly while the teacher or principal described the school's concern. If your parents and the school's staff exchanged ideas as equal participants in a problem-solving process, this was more the exception than the rule. Other attempts to involve your parents in your school experience were probably superficial and may have been planned to get them to rubber-stamp decisions the school had already made. These and other practices often alienated from the educational process the people with the greatest impact upon and the most profound knowledge of students—their parents.

Of course, many of these practices still remain, but in general parents today are more involved in their children's schooling than ever before in our nation's history. This trend is especially evident in special education. The passage of Public Law 94–142 gave a much needed boost to the practice of involving parents of special education children in their children's schooling by mandating their participation at virtually every step of the process. Indeed federal law spells out an active, decision-making role for you with the expectation that you will work in a partnership with school staff to develop and monitor your child's educational program. This chapter examines the various ways that you can take part, discusses some of the obstacles you may encounter along the way, and explores ways that you can overcome these obstacles. Special focus is placed on your role in developing the IEP.

USING YOUR EXPERTISE

You can use your expert knowledge of your child by

- *requesting a referral* for evaluation;
- *giving or withholding your written consent* to the preplacement

evaluation and the initial special education placement;

- *discussing your observations and concerns* during the evaluation and reevaluation process;
- *taking part in a meeting to discuss evaluation* results and special education eligibility status;
- *requesting an independent evaluation* because of dissatisfaction or disagreement with the school's evaluation;
- *helping to develop the IEP,* including your child's special education placement;
- *monitoring the educational program* to ensure its appropriateness;
- *supporting the special education program* through active and ongoing communication with teachers and reinforcement of program goals at home;
- *taking part in a formal review of IEP* at least once a year;
- *requesting an IEP review or reevaluation* of your child before the scheduled date;
- *examining your child's school records* and giving (or withholding) written consent for their release to persons outside the school system;
- *challenging school decisions* through informal procedures or a due-process hearing;
- *joining parent groups* and advocacy organizations;
- *taking part in local parent advisory council meetings* and in the development of the special education plan that must be drawn up each year by the local school district;
- *attending public hearings* on your state's required annual special education plan; and
- *joining the special education advisory panel* which each state is required to establish (and which must include at least one parent of a special education student).

This list is by no means exhaustive. In fact, some districts have established committees of parents and educators to interview prospective teachers, review special education programs, and suggest program changes. Your school district may not go so far, but in any case federal lawmakers have guaranteed opportunities for you to participate as equal partners in the special education process. What actually happens in your school district depends on your willingness to seize these opportunities, and the district's willingness to make your participation as free of obstacles as possible.

You as well as your child have much to gain from this involvement. Taking part in the educational planning process can help you understand your child's learning problems, provide appropriate academic and emotional support at home, and plan for the future. At the same time, it may give you greater skill and confidence in advocating for your child in future contacts with schools and other organizations. And finding that you are an effective advocate for your child can leave you feeling very good about yourself.

OBSTACLES TO YOUR INVOLVEMENT

Parents can play a critical role in the special education of their children, and the law guarantees opportunities for their involvement, yet studies show that many parents contribute minimally, if at all, to the planning process. Parents typically attend IEP conferences, but, believing that educators are the experts, many are content to accept without question the recommendations of school officials. The involvement of these parents is often limited to signing off on the IEP.

If you have been one of these parents, your attitude is not hard to understand. When you think about how *your* parents and their parents related to school, you probably realize that for you to assume an active, decision-making role goes against long entrenched patterns and is often an act of daring. While parents have exercised control over public schools by approving or disapproving school budgets and by electing board of education members, they have been reluctant to enter the arena of educational decision making. Some have reasoned that educational decisions are best left to the educators. Those willing to play a more substantial role were often intimidated at the prospect of confronting school administrators who used jargon they did not understand and who elicited an instinctive response of compliance reminding them of their own school days. Often parents were denied access to critical information. School staff, threatened by the prospect of parents usurping their decision-making prerogatives, may have viewed parents as uninformed persons to be tolerated, neutralized, or appeased, and often may have encouraged their more passive posture.

Parents and educators have made dramatic strides in their willingness and ability to work cooperatively, but as the parent of a special education student, you may continue to face some fairly steep barriers as you try to participate fully in decisions concerning your youngster (see Figure 5.1). Forming an effective partnership with the school may take a lot of energy and willingness to communicate on

FIGURE 5.1   **Obstacles to Parent Involvement in the Special Education Process**

Parent Beliefs/Actions	Educator Beliefs/Actions
Failure or inability to attend meetings with school personnel	Failure to make accommodations to ensure parents' attendance at meetings
Failure to become adequately informed about special education issues	Failure to provide parents with needed information to contribute effectively
Difficulty in asserting oneself with professionals or authority figures	Reacting to parents in cold, unsympathetic manner and projecting image of superiority and certainty
Lack of confidence in one's ability to contribute meaningfully to the process	Underestimation of the value of parent contributions
Belief that one's input will not be listened to or respected	Failure to elicit or consider parent perspective
Fear of "making waves"	Belief that parents' participation will result in confrontation with school or usurping of educators' decision-making prerogatives
Fear that school will treat child unfairly as a result of parents' assertiveness	Failure to assure parents of fair and unbiased treatment of children with special needs
Belief that educators have all the answers and should therefore make the decisions	Belief that parents do not want to be involved
Belief that one is too emotionally involved to be objective	Belief that parents are too emotionally involved and guilt-ridden to make sound educational decisions
Fear of being perceived as overanxious or overprotective	Intimation that parents are to blame for their child's learning problem
Belief, without full information, that the school is doing the best it can	Presentation of information in technical manner without explanation

both sides. Educators must recognize and use constructively your knowledge, commitment, and energy, while acknowledging the burdens you may bear. You, in turn, must be willing to state assertively your views and concerns while recognizing the constraints affecting educators.

What if you don't wish to play an active role? This is also your right. Some parents choose to participate minimally in the special education process even when potential obstacles have been removed. You may feel that you lack the time, skills, energy, or desire to serve as equal partners in the development and support of your child's special education program. You may need a break from the demands of parenting and may decide to leave educational planning up to the school. If this is your situation, do yourself the favor of making a conscious choice not to participate fully, rather than just telling yourself that you are too busy, or too inexperienced. And be clear about your decision. Just as school professionals should respect and accommodate those parents who wish to be active participants, so too must they respect your wishes if you choose to be minimally involved.

EFFECTIVE COMMUNICATION STRATEGIES

The partnership between parents and educators hinges on effective communication, on an honest exchange of views. You may already have strong communication skills, or you may find it useful to develop a range of skills and strategies that will help ensure that educators understand and consider the merits of your views. Some of the key components of effective communication are considered below.

Active Listening

First, it is helpful to recall that effective communication is a two-way street. Careful and attentive listening not only allows you to understand how other people think; it also conveys respect for the speaker and his or her message. Listening is an active process. If you are an active listener, you are likely to:

> turn your head to the speaker;
> maintain good eye contact;
> listen without interrupting;
> encourage the speaker (for example, through a simple "uh-huh" or a nod of the head);
> listen for the feelings behind the message; and
> observe the speaker's body language.

The more actively you listen to an educator, the more likely the educator will be to give your views an attentive and respectful hearing.

Asserting Your Viewpoint

Your role in the special education process is not limited to receiving information. You are expected to express your views and feelings—and not just as an exercise in democracy. The point is to see to it that your child gets the education you want for him or her. How you express your views may determine their impact on decisions that affect your son or daughter. With this in mind, you might give some thought to your own communication style. Three styles are often described by educators.

Assertive parents express their views and feelings in an honest, forthright, and calm manner while respecting the rights of others. Nonassertive parents express their views in a tentative and indirect manner or do not express them at all. They often consent to whatever the school proposes, in effect abdicating their decision-making role and risking violation of their own rights and those of their children. Nonassertive parents are often left with a sense of guilt, frustration, helplessness, and perhaps resentment. Aggressive parents express their views in a demanding, dominating, sometimes hostile manner without concern for the rights of others. Aggressive parents may succeed in obtaining their specific demands but risk alienating and losing the rapport with school staff that is critical to the program's ultimate success. Their victory will likely be short-lived.

The following situation and the sample responses highlight the differences among these communication styles. At an IEP meeting, school staff recommend that James, a recently evaluated second grader, be placed in a special education class for learning-disabled students, with mainstreaming only for gym and music classes. James's parents recognize their son's learning disability but prefer a less restrictive placement.

> The *assertive parent* might say: "I agree that James has a learning problem and needs special education help, but I'm not convinced that the program you've described is the right one for him, so at this point I'm not prepared to agree with the recommendation. It seems to me that there are some academic areas where James can keep up pretty well with other second graders. I'm interested in knowing about other options that would allow James to stay in his class and still get the extra help he needs."
>
> The *nonassertive parent* might say: "I'm not sure how James is going to react to this class but you're the experts so I guess

you know what's best. So if you're recommending this special class it's okay with me.''

The *aggressive parent* might say: "You give my child a few tests
and then you want to dump him in one of those 'retard'
classes. That's your way of getting him out of your hair. Well,
you don't know James like I know him. He can do a lot better than you say. No way is he going in that class.''

The assertive parent in this example clearly states his or her op-
position to the proposal, while maintaining rapport with school officials and keeping discussion headed toward a constructive solution.
Assertive parents generally tend to

respect and trust their own judgments;
ask questions about any issues they do not understand or request
    clarification of terms they don't know;
express their views in a polite, calm, but forthright manner;
restate their viewpoint when they think it is not being heard;
express appreciation to school staff when appropriate or ac-
    knowledge the difficulty of their work;
communicate a sense of cooperation ("How can we resolve that
    problem?");
avoid fault-finding, name-calling, or other judgmental comments,
    and use a minimum of "should" and "ought" statements;
request specific services or offer their own ideas about how to
    solve a problem;
request and examine various placement options before providing
    consent;
request an independent evaluation if they disagree with the
    school's evaluation;
be willing to disagree with a school's view of their children or its
    recommendations;
refuse to consent to a special education placement if they think it
    is inappropriate; and
confront school officials in a nonthreatening manner if they fail to
    fulfill their promises or obligations.

Sticking up for yourself, or your child, is not a simple task. If
communicating in an assertive manner does not come easily to you,
rest assured that you are like many other parents. Fortunately, it is a
skill that can be learned (just as nonassertiveness is learned). If you
think you could be a more effective advocate for your child, you might

consider one of the "assertiveness training" courses available in mental health centers, adult schools, or universities. Or, you might check your library for one of the many available books which describe systematic and practical approaches to becoming more assertive. *Parents Are to Be Seen AND Heard*, described at the end of this chapter, is particularly good. Developing these skills will not only help ensure that your youngster will receive an appropriate and effective education, but also may help you deal more effectively with organizations other than the school systems.

Understanding the School Setting

Effective communication requires a grasp of the system in which you are working. A school system, like any other bureaucracy, has standard policies and procedures that you need to recognize and understand if you are to find your way through the special education maze. While this brief section cannot do justice to the "culture" of the school, it highlights some aspects of most school systems.

It's all well and good to know how to communicate, but with whom should you be doing this communicating? Knowing this requires an understanding of the school's organizational structure or "chain of command." While the personnel structure of a school district varies with its size and its priorities (other parents or school staff may be able to provide information about school organization in your district), the following is a typical special education hierarchy, arranged from the ground up—from the classroom level to the next level of authority:

> special education teacher
> principal
> director of special education (or special services)
> superintendent
> local board of education
> county and/or state departments of special education
> state commissioner of education

As a rule, contact the teacher first with any concerns about your child, and then move to the next level if you are not satisfied with the response. Going over the heads of school staff (for example, by calling the superintendent to request an evaluation before speaking with anyone else) may alienate the people with whom you will need to work

cooperatively. But you should not hesitate to climb this ladder a rung
at a time to pursue deeply felt concerns.

The more you know about the workings of your school district (for
example, how decisions are made, who makes them, what constraints
affect the teacher and other school staff, what political issues may stir
strong feelings), the more effective you can be as an advocate for your
child. Other parents can often help you get a feeling for these issues.

Developing a File

As your daughter or son goes through school, you will attend
many meetings, make and receive many phone calls, and accumulate
a tall stack of documents. Effective advocacy requires that you keep
careful track of these communications, either through a file or notebook. A comprehensive well-organized file can help you identify patterns and discrepancies in your child's learning and behavioral
characteristics, keep track of progress (or lack of progress), prepare
for the IEP meeting and other school contacts, and obtain an appropriate educational program with little delay if you move to a new
school district. The file's contents can provide the documentation you
may need to justify your requests for services and to hold the school
district accountable for its obligations.

To begin your home file, review your child's school file and request copies of any documents you wish to include. You can also request copies of reports completed by professionals outside the school
district (for example, physicians). Your file should be kept in chronological order and may include

- medical and developmental history;
- state and federal special education laws;
- names, addresses, and telephone numbers of organizations as
  well as individuals;
- your own notes about your child's strengths and weaknesses,
  likes and dislikes, and learning and behavioral characteristics;
- report cards, progress reports, and samples of schoolwork (with
  completion dates);
- your own notes about problems encountered in school and solutions that worked or didn't work;
- evaluation reports and IEPs;
- questions asked of professionals and their responses;
- notes of visits to special education programs;

- notes of telephone calls and conferences with school staff or other professionals, including dates, person(s) contacted, purpose, and results;
- letters sent and received;
- calendar for the school year with dates that actions are to be taken by you or the school; and
- articles you have clipped, or any information that is relevant to your child's schooling.

THE IEP MEETING

The most important school meeting you are likely to attend is the IEP meeting. At this meeting, you and school staff develop your child's special education program. There are a number of strategies you can use to prepare for and participate in this meeting. Many of these strategies apply to other school meetings as well.

Preparing for the IEP Meeting

- *Clarify the nature of the meeting.* Find out in advance the meeting's agenda, how long it will last, and who will attend. You may wish to request the presence of other school staff or suggest that more time be allocated.
- *Become familiar with your child's learning and behavioral characteristics.* Observe your child in different situations at home (for example, interacting with peers, completing homework, following directions, and playing games). Consider going to school sometime before the meeting to observe your child in class (giving the school advanced notification). Review samples of the schoolwork. These steps can help you pinpoint strengths and weaknesses.
- *Review written information.* Go over the various documents you have accumulated (for example, evaluation reports, IEPs, and progress reports), jot down information relevant to your child's present educational status, and select those you want to bring to the meeting.
- *Talk with your child.* Ask questions that will aid you in developing an educational program appropriate to his or her needs. Probe gently to find out such information as subjects and activities your child likes or dislikes in school, perceptions of strengths

and weaknesses, conditions under which he or she learns best, and suggestions for program changes.

• *Talk with other parents.* Other parents who have attended IEP meetings can guide you in what will be discussed and decided at the meeting, how to participate effectively, and what you need to know about the school policies and procedures. Parent organizations (for example, the Association for Children and Adults with Learning Disabilities) can also be helpful.

• *Review evaluation reports.* Request from the school reports of all of the most recent evaluations. These evaluations will form the basis for the IEP, so going over them and thinking about their implications will help you contribute to the IEP meeting. In reviewing these reports, jot down questions as well as points of agreement and disagreement.

• *Review state and federal special education regulations.* Become familiar with the IEP—its various parts and the process for its development. Other parents and parent organizations can help you make sense of the regulations.

• *Consider what you want included in the IEP.* After you've gone through some or all of the above steps, write down your own ideas about:

your child's strengths and weaknesses;
specific skills and concepts you want your child to learn—perhaps in the form of goals and objectives, as described in chapter 4;
program placement and related services you believe are necessary to meet your child's educational needs (described in chapter 4);
approaches that are effective and ineffective in teaching, motivating, and disciplining your child; and
subjects and school activities in which your child should participate with children who do not have disabilities.

You may write out your thoughts and preferences in some detail, or you may just jot down your ideas. This will depend, of course, on your own style of operating. In any case, do think about what you want to accomplish at an IEP meeting.

• *Write out a list of any questions you may have.* Bring them to the meeting.

• *Consider bringing another person with you to the meeting.* Your guest—a relative, friend, another parent experienced in the IEP process, a therapist, or an advocate—may have special education expertise or knowledge of your child, provide support to you or your child, and help you to raise important issues and questions. Parent organizations may provide advocates who will accompany you under special circumstances. Notify the school in advance if you intend to bring someone with you. If a person is unable to attend (for example, your family doctor), you may bring along his or her written statements to share with school staff.

• *Think about whether your child should attend the meeting, or some part of it.* Discuss the pros and cons with school staff and with your child. Children should participate in IEP meetings more often than they do. Their perceptions are often insightful and can be valuable in designing specific aspects of the educational program. Your child may be more receptive to an educational program that he or she has helped to design; adolescents are especially likely to resist programs they feel are imposed on them without their input. Consider whether your child will be more comfortable in a smaller, less formal meeting and whether he or she should attend all or only part of the meeting.

You might prepare your child for the meeting by helping him or her to understand its purpose and format and the specific issues to be discussed. Talk over any questions your child may want to ask or may be asked. Encourage your youngster to write down—if appropriate—questions or ideas for discussion at the meeting. Having your child make a specific and concrete list of positive and negative aspects of school, as well as things he or she would like to learn, may be helpful. It may also be useful to role-play your child's involvement in the meeting.

• *Rehearse your part in the meeting.* If you don't have much experience at formal meetings—or even if you do—you may want to practice telling someone the points you want to get across at the meeting and responding to proposals presented by the school staff.

Participating in the IEP Meeting

If you have taken some of the steps suggested above, you will be well prepared to contribute to the IEP meeting. The following tips will help to ensure that your contributions are well received and that they are reflected in the IEP.

- *Attend the meeting.* The school may give you the option of discussing the IEP over the phone. Say no. It is essential that you appear in person (and that both parents attend if possible). A phone call is usually not adequate for exploring the often complex issues and making the important decisions that the IEP process requires.
- *Find a seat that allows you to participate easily.* You may prefer to sit next to someone with whom you feel comfortable. Make sure, however, that you don't distance yourself from the "action."
- *Consider taking notes.* This not only provides a record of what was discussed but may help focus your concentration and enhance the participation of others. Review your notes before the meeting's end and ask for clarification where necessary. You can also record the meeting (as can the school district), but you should balance the benefits of having a verbatim record against the tape recorder's potentially inhibiting effect upon the discussion. The law considers a tape recording of an IEP meeting by the school district to be an "education record" to which you must be given access.
- *Ask for clarification.* The special education maze can perplex the most sophisticated of parents. Do not accept the notion, however, that evaluation results or special education practices are too complex for you to understand. Request an explanation whenever you do not understand terms, acronyms, concepts, procedural and legal issues, and program options. Ask for examples, if necessary. You might also restate what another person has said to make sure you're on the same wavelength.
- *Keep the discussion focused on your child and the program.* If discussion wanders off onto unrelated topics, try to bring it back to your child's educational needs and the program implications.
- *Check out your child's reactions.* If you child is present, make sure he or she has an opportunity to contribute to the program's design and to react to any recommendations. Your daughter or son may not be accustomed to participating in school conferences and may require some gentle probing.
- *Make sure all aspects of the IEP are discussed.* Make a list of the required components and the optional items you want included (as described in chapter 4) and check them off as they are discussed.
- *Inquire about the various placement options and ask to observe them.* Observing special education placement options (while

school is in session) can help you make an informed decision about the educational program. You may want your child to go with you so you can gauge his or her reactions. Use the guidelines described in chapter 4 ("Selecting a Placement") to help evaluate the placements.

• *Ask for suggestions about home activities.* Find out what you can do to support the program and help your child. These activities may even be incorporated into the IEP. Educators usually respond well to parents who are willing to assume some responsibility for their child's education.

• *Try to resolve areas of disagreement.* This is what the IEP process was designed to do. After agreeing about where your disagreements lie, identify those areas you feel are negotiable and those that are not. Discuss each item separately and try to reach a solution acceptable to all, recognizing that the school will prevail in some cases and you in others. But remember that you and the school district are under no obligation to compromise; each can pursue a due-process hearing to seek resolution of a disagreement.

• *Request a copy of the IEP.* You are entitled to a copy of this document (and most districts will give you a copy as a matter of course). You can refer to your copy throughout the year to keep track of your child's progress and the school's fulfillment of its obligations.

• *Consider requesting a follow-up meeting.* One meeting may be inadequate to discuss all aspects of the IEP or to arrive at a program agreeable to all parties.

Deciding Whether to Consent

At the end of the IEP meeting, a school official will probably ask you to consent in writing to the special education program. Some districts have a separate consent form while others put a signature line right on the IEP. You should think carefully about the consent decision: remember that once you sign, the school district must provide all services described on the IEP, but cannot be obliged to provide any special education service not in the document until a new IEP is developed.

You may feel pressured to consent right away, but there is no need for you to respond immediately to a school official's request. You may want to take the IEP home, go over it carefully, and discuss it with others before deciding whether to consent. As a matter of courtesy, you should let the school district know when you expect to make a decision. You can use the checklist in figure 5.2 to decide whether the IEP meets legal standards and describes an appropriate program tailored to your child's educational needs. While most IEPs will lack some of the items found on this checklist, the more items complied with, the greater confidence you can have in the document's soundness. A significant number of negative responses suggests that the IEP—and the program that would result from it—are inappropriate.

When you think over the consent decision, keep in mind the school district's obligation to provide to all identified children with special needs an "appropriate" educational program. A district cannot deny an eligible child an appropriate program for any reason, including the following:

- There is no room in the program.
- The school district does not have the proper program for the child.
- The school district lacks adequate funds to provide the program.
- The school district does not provide special education programs for students who have that kind of problem or who are of that age level (assuming the student is of public school age).
- The school district does not have a teacher qualified to teach the student.

Once you consent to the program, the district must begin implementing it as soon as possible. If you agree with the placement in general, but disagree with particular aspects of the program (for example, the number of speech therapy sessions per week), you can consent to the placement and authorize its implementation while indicating on the consent form the specific area of disagreement. You can then challenge this aspect of the program without delaying the basic services your child needs. If, on the other hand, you disagree with the placement itself, you can withhold your consent altogether. If you withhold consent to the initial special education placement, you and the school district may agree upon an alternative program or either party may initiate a due-process hearing. Your child remains in his or her current program until the dispute is resolved, unless an interim placement can be agreed upon.

FIGURE 5.2   IEP Checklist

This checklist can help you evaluate whether the IEP written for your child conforms with federal regulations, and whether it meets your youngster's educational needs. Answer each question by putting a check in the "Yes" or "No" column. (Please note that in several questions, the term "special services" refers to special education and related services.) Keep in mind that while the items mentioned are not all required by law, they do make for a better, more effective IEP. When you review the completed checklist, the more checks you find in the "Yes" column, the more confident you can be that the IEP is an effective educational plan.

YES	NO	
☐	☐	1. Was the IEP meeting held within thirty days of the determination of your youngster's special education eligibility?
☐	☐	2. Was the meeting attended by all the persons who are required by law to take part in developing the IEP?
☐	☐	3. Was the IEP developed at the IEP meeting (rather than by school staff before the meeting took place)?
☐	☐	4. Was the IEP developed *before* your child's special education program took effect?
☐	☐	5. Were you actively involved in writing the IEP?
☐	☐	6. Was the possibility of including your child at the IEP meeting discussed ahead of time?
☐	☐	7. Does the IEP contain all of the components required by federal law, including: —your child's current educational status; —annual goals and short-term objectives; —special education and related services which the school district will provide; —a statement defining the degree to which your youngster will participate in the regular education program; —the proposed date for beginning the program; —a statement about how long the special education and related services will last; —specific methods and a schedule for evaluating your youngster's progress in the areas of special education instruction?
☐	☐	8. Does the IEP include any other features required by the laws of your state? (The division of special education of your state department of education can inform you of these requirements.)
☐	☐	9. Does the description of the current educational status in the IEP give a specific, objective account of your child's present learning and behavioral characteristics with minimal use of labels?

☐ ☐ 10. Does the current educational status section describe skills and concepts which your child has mastered and not mastered in all areas in which special services are required?

☐ ☐ 11. Does the current educational status section describe the effect of the disability on your child's performance in academic and nonacademic areas?

☐ ☐ 12. Are the annual goals and objectives written for each area in which your child is scheduled to receive special services?

☐ ☐ 13. Are the annual goals consistent with the description of your youngster's current educational status?

☐ ☐ 14. Can each annual goal be achieved realistically within one year?

☐ ☐ 15. Has each of the annual goals been broken down into short-term objectives?

☐ ☐ 16. Do the goals and objectives indicate specific levels of expected performance to enable objective evaluation of whether they have been attained?

☐ ☐ 17. Does the IEP indicate all the special services that your child will need in order to meet the stated goals and objectives?

☐ ☐ 18. Does the IEP clearly spell out the amount and/or frequency of the special services?

☐ ☐ 19. Are the proposed special services based on your child's unique educational needs rather than on classification or type of disability?

☐ ☐ 20. Is the proposed placement the least restrictive educational setting in light of your youngster's learning and behavioral characteristics?

☐ ☐ 21. Is the proposed setting as close to home as possible?

☐ ☐ 22. Is the proposed setting free of architectural barriers that would keep your child from taking full part in the educational program?

☐ ☐ 23. Does the IEP describe the extent to which your youngster will take part in the regular education program?

☐ ☐ 24. Does the IEP describe modifications, including alternative testing procedures, that will make it possible for your child to take part in the regular education program?

☐ ☐ 25. Does the IEP describe, if appropriate, a specially designed physical or vocational education program or

continued

Figure 5.2 *continued*

modifications necessary in the regular physical or vocational education programs?

☐ ☐ 26. Does the IEP indicate specialized instructional materials and aids as well as any equipment needed to enhance your child's learning?

☐ ☐ 27. Does the IEP describe specific teaching methods and strategies appropriate to your child's learning and behavioral characteristics?

☐ ☐ 28. Does the IEP name the people responsible for carrying out the various aspects of your child's program?

☐ ☐ 29. Does the IEP include specific and objective procedures and a timetable for evaluating your youngster's attainment of goals and objectives?

☐ ☐ 30. Can you use the IEP easily to check your child's progress?

☐ ☐ 31. Are the evaluation procedures practical? Can they be carried out efficiently, without undue distress to your child or disruption of his or her school life?

☐ ☐ 32. Does the IEP indicate when the special services are to begin and how long they are to continue?

☐ ☐ 33. Does the IEP reflect your views as well as those of the teacher and other school staff?

COMMUNICATING WITH THE TEACHER

Consent to the special education placement opens up new opportunities for you to participate in your child's educational program. The most important step you can take is to establish an effective working relationship with your child's main teachers (as well as other school staff such as a guidance counselor or speech therapist with whom your youngster may work closely). In short, you can help form a coalition of the adults most influential in your child's education. By forging a relationship founded on respect, equality, open communication, and an understanding of each other's pressures and constraints, you and the teacher(s) can combine expertise to anticipate problems and resolve them at the earliest stages. Ongoing communication with the teacher also enables you to closely monitor your child's progress and the appropriateness of the educational program.

If the IEP results in a new teacher for your child, try to meet with him or her before the program begins, or soon after. If your child has more than one teacher, meet with those who will most need to understand your child's characteristics in order to modify their instruction.

This initial meeting will probably leave lasting impressions and prepare the groundwork for future cooperation, so it should be positive and friendly in tone. It provides an opportunity for you and the teacher to get to know each other, to exchange information and expectations, and generally to open up communication. You may want to share information about your child's disability that is not contained in the IEP (for example, how to use specialized equipment or recent changes in the home situation). You might also ask about how the program is being individualized to meet your child's needs, such as the· modification of test-taking, grading, and homework assignments. You may also explore with the teacher opportunities for your direct involvement in the class (for example, as a room parent, classroom aide, chaperone, or coordinator of a special project or activity). If it is feasible for you to serve as a classroom aide, this will allow you to see your child in an academic setting and learn strategies for working with him or her by observing the teacher. When you review your child's work or observe him or her in class, keep in mind that the instruction should reflect the goals and objectives stated in the IEP.

Your communication with the teacher should be ongoing. While the nature and frequency of these contacts will vary widely, here is an example of a parent-teacher meeting schedule:

Meeting 1 (Beginning of the School Year). Introduction, exchange of information and expectations, and establishment of formal or informal communication system.

Meeting 2 (Mid-November). Teacher assessment of child's strengths and weaknesses, review of progress, exchange of information and suggestions, and joint problem resolution.

Meeting 3 (Mid-March). Same tasks as meeting 2.

Meeting 4 (Early June). Review of year's progress, discussion of program for following year, discussion of child's summer activities. This meeting may be supplanted by the IEP review meeting.

Meeting face-to-face is always a good idea, but other kinds of communication are useful as well. Some parents and teachers arrange to talk by phone on a regular basis; others send notes, a notebook, or a weekly folder back and forth with the child (the lunch box is a convenient place for notes).

FIGURE 5.3   Daily Report Card

Student: Teacher: Week:

INSTRUCTIONS: Rate the student using the definitions below by giving
                points as follows:

    1 = Poor   2 = Fair   3 = Good   4 = Excellent

SCALE:

	Monday	Tuesday	Wednesday	Thursday	Friday
Seatwork Completion					
Homework Completion					
Classroom Behavior					
Teacher Initials					
Parent Initials					

DEFINITIONS: Define more specifically each of the following areas to
               guide student in knowing how to perform and teacher in
               how to evaluate student.

    Seatwork Completion:

    Homework Completion:

    Classroom Behavior:

COMMENTS (Optional):   Use to elaborate on student's performance, note
                       changes in school/home situation, make suggestions
                       to parents or teacher,etc. Note date of comments.
                       Use other side if needed.

Teacher   Parents

Some children have educational problems that call for particularly frequent home-school contact. An alternative to regular phone
contact or handwritten notes is a daily report card, as shown in figure
5.3. This daily summary of the child's school performance is com-

pleted by the teacher, brought home by your child for your review and signature, and returned the following day; both you and the teacher have the option of writing comments. It is a quick and efficient communication device that can help you monitor your child's progress. It can also be used as part of a behavior modification program in which you provide incentives when your child attains a specified number of points. The form can be modified to suit your child's needs (for example, by pinpointing behaviors that need improvement such as "following directions" or "classroom participation").

COMMUNICATING WITH YOUR CHILD

Your son or daughter may be confused by the learning problem and distressed by a program change, particularly if it means attending a new class or school. Middle and high school students, who are often occupied with peer perceptions, may be especially concerned about their special education status. Here are examples of concerns your child may have:

Why can't I learn as well as other kids? Is something wrong with me?
Will I ever be in a regular class again?
What if I fail the special program?
What grade will I be in?
Why do I have to ride the "retard" bus?
Can I still be on the baseball team?
What should I do if other kids tease me?
What do I tell my friends about my new program?
Will I be able to graduate from high school? Get a job? Go to college?

Try to anticipate some of these concerns and talk about them openly with your child. You need to walk a fine line, though, between discussing the program changes in such a serious, dramatic way that you alarm your child, and discussing them in such a casual and superficial way that you unwittingly perpetuate your youngster's fears. You'll want to talk over your child's learning problem and the program change in a way that he or she will understand, considering age and conceptual ability (concrete examples may be helpful), but in any case candor and honesty are essential. Children, including those with learning problems, are often quick to see through half-truths and evasions. Statements such as "we all have a disability of some kind" are likely to be of little comfort. Providing false hopes (for example, "You'll probably only need to be in the class for a couple of months," or "If you work hard, you'll be able to catch up with the others in a year or two") may relieve your child in the short run, but can result in long-term anger and resentment if the hope is not realized. At the same time, avoid suggesting to your child that the challenges may prove too much to handle. This can become a self-fulfilling prophesy: conveying to your child through your words or actions that he or she may not be able to cope can give rise to self-doubt, timidity, and apprehension.

Use a communication style with which you are comfortable, but avoid lecturing. Give your child a chance to express concerns and do not dismiss them as foolish. Gentle probing may be necessary to elicit worries your child is reluctant to share. Try to address each concern in a realistic but reassuring way. If necessary, speak with a school staff member to find out answers to your child's questions. Your child will probably need your help to place his or her learning problem and program change in perspective. Special education students are often preoccupied with their weakness and may need to be reminded of areas, either academic or nonacademic, in which they perform well. Your youngster may be surprised—and relieved—to find out that most children experience difficulty in some academic area and that many need special help. You may want to share some of your own academic struggles or those of prominent people (such as Bruce Jenner, the Olympic decathlon champion, who had a reading problem). If your child cannot relate to these examples, he or she might respond better to hearing of a peer's experience with a similar learning problem. It is also important to let your child know that these problems can often be overcome, or compensated for, with appropriate educational programs. You may also want to talk with your other children to enlist their understanding and support.

Despite your reassurances, your child may continue to agonize over the program change. These concerns will probably fade in intensity soon after the new program begins, when your child finds the work less frustrating than in the previous setting, experiences success, and establishes friendships. Peer ridicule may, however, pose a continuing problem. You can help your child by listening attentively and empathetically and helping to develop specific strategies for responding (or not responding) to teasing. You might elicit suggestions from your child ("What might you do or say if . . . ?) and then offer feedback about how effective that response is likely to be. If the problem persists, alert the teacher or another supervising adult to the situation, or encourage your child to speak up.

What you say—and how you say it—can significantly shape your child's perceptions and his or her response to the placement. If you do not understand the rationale for the special education program or are not convinced of its need, you will probably communicate your confusion or ambivalence; your child may interpret your uneasiness as disappointment, or may take it to be implicit permission to slack off or perhaps even undermine the program's success. The implication is clear: make sure you understand the need for the special education services and are comfortable with the recommendation before consenting to the program and explaining it to your child.

PARENT SUPPORT AND ADVOCACY

The experience of raising a child with a disability can be completely understood only by those who have gone through it. Parents may experience a range of reactions, including denial, anger, relief, hopelessness, exhilaration, fear, pride, and acceptance. The process can be physically as well as emotionally taxing. The routines of daily family life—shopping, doing laundry, socializing, getting together with other families in the neighborhood, going on vacations, and so on—are rarely routine and frequently ridden with problems. Tasks that many parents take for granted, such as arranging a car pool or finding a babysitter, can be ordeals for the parents of a child with special needs. They may also expend much energy, time, money, and emotion in obtaining needed services—educational, psychological, and medical—and in dealing with professionals. In their preoccupation with trying to meet their child's needs, parents may neglect their own needs and forget that they too have rights that must be respected. (See Figure 5.4.) The demands of parenting a child with special needs can place intense stress on the family, with siblings resentful of parents' diverted attention and necessary sacrifice, and the parents' own relationship strained.

While these strains may be particularly evident in families with children who have severe disabilities, the experience of raising a child with a less severe disability can bring a different kind of challenge. Parents whose children have such problems as minimal brain dysfunction, a specific learning disability, or a perceptual handicap may experience painful uncertainty as they try to grasp the nature and cause of an invisible and bewildering condition. They may find their hopes being alternately raised and dashed and their emotions being tugged in a variety of directions by conflicting professional opinions and confusing signals from their child.

FIGURE 5.4   A Bill of Rights for Parents

Parents of special education students are acutely aware of their responsibilities to provide educational, medical, emotional, and professional help for their off-spring, but are seldom aware of the rights they also have as parents of a child with a handicap, and as just plain people. Remember: you too have rights. These include the right to

- Love and enjoy your child.
- Feel that you have done the best you can.
- Be depressed or have hostile thoughts once in a while without feeling guilty.
- Be guilty occasionally, but only if it organizes you.
- Not always feel you have to be patient.
- Enjoy life as intensely as possible, even though you have a child who is handicapped.
- Have interesting causes to support and to be busier than the average person, to a point where people say, "How does he (or she) do it?" (If you want something done, ask a busy person.)
- Let your handicapped child have his or her own private life.
- Enjoy being alone at times.
- Get away for at least a two-week vacation every year without the children.
- Have dates, anniversaries, celebrations, weekends away, time together designed to enhance your marriage or "singlehood"—in other words, freedom for escapist moments.
- Have a sense of humor without feeling guilty.
- Acknowledge you are spending lots of time with your child without having it mean you love the rest of the family less.
- Not devote your entire life to the "cause," but freedom to devote as much as you want or to get away for a while.
- Say at times that you don't want to talk about your problem.
- Let people know at other times about the progress and achievements with a genuine sense of pride.
- Lie every once in a while, to say everything is fine, not feeling compelled to tell the truth to everyone who asks, "How are you?"
- Tell teachers and other professionals how you really feel about the job they are doing, and to demand they respect your opinions.
- Tell your child that you don't like certain things he or she does regardless of the presence of a handicap.
- Not praise your child gratuitously, even though you've been told to offer a lot of praise.
- Spend a little extra money on yourself, whether or not you can afford it.
- Have your hobbies and interests without interference—whether Majong, Mahler, or macrame.

Source: Adapted from "A Bill of Rights for Parents" by S. Gordon, 1976, *Academic Therapy, II*, pp. 21—22. Copyright by Academic Therapy. Reprinted by permission.

You may find the support of others helpful in your efforts to raise and educate your child. You may need emotional support to allow you to ventilate your feelings and to sort through them; you may need information to help you understand various aspects of your child's disability, its educational implications, and the special education system; and you may need help learning skills with which you can effectively care for your child and represent his or her educational interests. The need for support may be heightened at specific milestones in your child's education—the initial special education placement, for example, or the beginning of secondary school, or graduation.

While a variety of professionals and organizations offer services to meet these needs (some states, for example, have organizations devoted to training parents of children with disabilities in the special education process), many parents have benefited from their interaction with other parents who have gone through similar experiences. These contacts can give you a chance to share your concerns, questions, struggles, and successes with people who may be able to identify closely with your situation; they can reassure you that other parents experience similar, or perhaps even more trying, emotional struggles and physical rigors. You may be relieved to hear, for example, that other parents also feel anger and resentment toward their children. And you may be relieved to share your small day-to-day triumphs with people who can appreciate their significance and will not respond with the patronizing smiles that may come your way all too often. Other parents can also provide a gold mine of experience-based information about raising a child with special needs, negotiating the bureaucratic maze, and obtaining hard-to-find services. Hearing how other parents solved problems may suggest solutions to problems you are facing.

Parents of children with disabilities have been instrumental in establishing what is now an extensive network of organizations to serve support as well as advocacy purposes. These groups may be local chapters of national organizations (for example, the Association for Children and Adults with Learning Disabilities or the Association for Retarded Citizens) or they may be entirely local (for example, a special education PTA). The groups may be organized to accommodate the needs and constraints of the parents in the district; the district's director of special education or special services can probably provide information about them. Parent groups can

> arrange speakers on topics of interest to members;
> train you in particular educational or parenting skills;
> run "rap" groups for parents;

organize social groups for parents;

organize a resource network: a newsletter, a telephone hotline, listing of services such as babysitters;

arrange visits to other educational programs;

represent parents' concerns about local school district practices and develop advocacy strategies (for example, by making a presentation to the board of education); and

sponsor social or recreational programs for youngsters or young adults who have disabilities.

You can choose to advocate on behalf of your child at the state and national level. Indeed, by joining hands and combining their voices in the form of parent groups and coalitions, parents can play—and have played—a prominent role in the shaping of state and federal policy toward children with disabilities. In fact, the passage of Public Law 94–142 was largely due to the vigorous advocacy efforts of parent organizations. Important gains have been made, but these watchdog groups need ongoing support to ensure that the abuses of the past do not recur, that federal and state safeguards remain in place, and that local school districts comply with the letter and the spirit of the law and provide adequate funds and services. When the federal government wanted to eliminate some important procedural safeguards in 1981, parent groups mobilized to help preserve those regulations. You too can make a difference.

FOR FURTHER INFORMATION

The following is a sample of reading material on various aspects of raising, educating, and advocating for children who have disabilities.

ACLD summer camp directory for children with learning disabilities. Pittsburgh, Pa.: Association for Children and Adults with Learning Disabilities. (See Appendix B for publisher's address.)

Des Jardins, C. (1971). *How to organize an effective parent/advocacy group and move bureaucracies.* Chicago: Coordinating Council for Handicapped Children (CCHC). This 130-page book provides specific, practical information for starting and maintaining parent groups, from how to recruit volunteers to how to lobby effectively. (Address of CCHC in Appendix B.)

Gottesman, D. M. (1982). *The powerful parent—A child advocacy handbook.* Norwalk, Conn.: Appleton-Century-Crofts. Practical advice on how to obtain educational, medical, psychological, and legal services for your child.

Markel, G. P., and Greenbaum, J. (1979). *Parents are to be seen AND heard: Assertiveness in educational planning for handicapped children.* San Luis Obispo, Calif.: Impact. A systematic guide to assertive behavior with school officials in planning your child's IEP.

Murphy, A. T. (1980). *Special children, special parents: Personal issues with handicapped children.* Englewood Cliffs, N.J.: Prentice-Hall. Using first-hand accounts by parents of children with disabilities, this book explores personal issues faced by parents and offers coping strategies.

Osman, B. B. (1979). *Learning disabilities: A family affair.* New York: Random House. An educational therapist discusses, with warmth and sensitivity, the obstacles faced by learning-disabled children and their families, and offers coping strategies.

Stevens, S. (1980). *The learning-disabled child: Ways that parents can help.* Winston-Salem, N.C.: John F. Blair. Written by an experienced teacher, this short, easy-to-use handbook provides a wealth of practical information.

The Exceptional Parent. An information-packed magazine published six times per year for parents of children who have disabilities. To subscribe, contact *The Exceptional Parent,* 605 Commonwealth Ave., Boston, Mass. 02215; tel. 1-617-536-8961.

Turnbull, A. P., and Turnbull, H. R. (1978). *Parents speak out: Views from the other side of the two-way mirror.* Columbus, Ohio:

Charles E. Merrill. Written by professionals working in the field of special education who are also parents of children who have disabilities, this book describes the often frustrating experiences of dealing with the professionals and agencies that provide services for persons with disabilities.

Zang, B., ed. (1980). *How to get help for kids: A reference guide to services for handicapped children.* Syracuse, N.Y.: Gaylord.

6

Special Education in Practice

Your involvement in your child's education need not stop at the classroom door. While the classroom teacher is—and should be—your youngster's primary academic instructor, you can play a vital role in fostering your child's academic growth by reinforcing and supporting the teacher's efforts. Since a firm grasp of special education's basic principles and practices can help you to do this effectively, this chapter highlights specific (and necessarily selective) aspects of the process of teaching students who have disabilities.

THE ABCs OF INSTRUCTION

Like other teachers, special education teachers are most effective when they follow basic principles of instruction. Decades of research and practical experience have shown educators that students are likely to attend to, understand, and retain classroom instruction most successfully when

> they have a positive relationship with their teacher characterized by mutual esteem;
>
> the setting and structure of their classroom are conducive to learning;
>
> they actively participate in the lesson and can relate the task to their own experience;
>
> the instructional materials are appropriate to their conceptual and reading levels;
>
> they have opportunities to observe and model appropriate skills (both academic and social) of their teacher and their peers;
>
> they receive frequent feedback on their performance and positive reinforcement for their efforts and successes;
>
> they have opportunities to practice, review, and apply what they have learned;

they are encouraged, to the extent they are able, to rely less on
   the teacher and more on themselves in the learning process;
they are encouraged to think creatively; and
their academic progress is monitored periodically and the program is revised accordingly.

These principles form the bedrock of any successful special education program. Special educators build on this foundation through a
continuous process of educational matchmaking, trying to link a child's
learning and behavioral characteristics with the appropriate instructional programs, strategies, and materials. This process of individual-
izing instruction, which assumes that different children respond best
to different teaching approaches, is the hallmark of special education.

Remediating Academic Problems

The variety of teaching approaches used with special education
students—and there are many—generally fall into two categories:
process-oriented or task-oriented. The process-oriented approach (also
called the ability-training model) involves the development of perceptual, perceptual-motor, or linguistic skills that are assumed to be pre-
requisites for the development of academic skills. The task-oriented
approach (also called the direct-skill approach) involves the remediation of an academic task—that is, helping a student grasp the component skills of a task that has not yet been mastered. These two
approaches are discussed below in the context of reading instruction,
but they can be applied to other kinds of instruction as well.

Underlying most process-oriented approaches is the theory that
before your child can master a higher-order cognitive skill such as
reading, he or she must first develop more basic psychological abilities. A teacher may use process-oriented approaches in the hope that
building or reinforcing these more basic skills will boost academic
performance. Other professionals use this approach as well. For example, many optometrists offer perceptual training programs to students with reading problems on the assumption that improved visual-
perceptual skills will lead to improved academic skills. These and
similar approaches have generally failed to live up to their promise,
however. Studies have not shown definitively that perceptual or perceptual-motor skills training will bolster your youngster's academic
performance.

Task-oriented approaches, with their stress on the academic task
itself, have generally proven more effective. A teacher using this ap-

proach with David, who has a reading disability, would first assess his mastery of the various skills that go into reading (such as associating a symbol with its corresponding sound) and then choose particular strategies best suited to strengthening the skills that are weak.

A teacher can choose from a long menu of task-oriented approaches. If Melissa has a severe reading problem, for example, her teacher might use the Fernald Kinesthetic Method: the teacher tries to help Melissa retain letters and words by presenting them through various sensory modalities. Using the pathways of sight, hearing, and touch reinforces her retention of letters and letter patterns. Melissa first traces a sequence of letters with her finger, pronouncing each part of the word as she moves through it. She repeats this until she can write the word from memory. In the next stage, she looks at a word presented by the teacher, pronounces it, and tries to write it from memory. Gradually, she is exposed to words from standard texts and asked to repeat the look-say-write sequence. When she masters this skill, Melissa moves on to vocabulary development and comprehension.

In determining an appropriate teaching approach, the teacher must always keep in mind a child's learning characteristics. If Seth has poor auditory skills (he has difficulty, for example, hearing the sounds in words), he will probably not profit much from a phonics approach (which requires the ability to discriminate among sounds), but will benefit more from an approach that emphasizes the visual characteristics of words and the context clues of a sentence. If Matthew has visual-perceptual difficulties (so that, for example, he cannot always distinguish between such words as *spot* and *pots* or *bend* and *band*), he will probably benefit from an auditory approach to reading which stresses learning to blend sounds. In practice, of course, the instruction given to both Seth and Matthew involves visual *and* auditory aspects. The question here is one of emphasis.

As you can imagine, reading instruction is more complex than this limited discussion suggests. The important point is that in any area, for any disability, the special education teacher should be applying instructional strategies geared to a child's strengths and weaknesses, as well as his or her sensory characteristics. This does not mean that the teacher invents the wheel every morning and afternoon. Often, personalizing instruction means modifying existing educational approaches, not thinking up new ones.

This is where you come in. You can help the teacher make this match between your child's characteristics and the most appropriate instructional strategies by observing your youngster's efforts in activities that are directly or indirectly related to academic skills (doing homework, for example, or reading a comic book), and noticing the conditions that seem to foster effective learning. Does your child

learn best through seeing or hearing information?

retain concepts best when he or she uses and manipulates concrete materials?

understand certain concepts best by experiencing them through movement?

work best with quiet or with background noise?

respond better to small-group or one-to-one instruction?

need the parameters of an assignment—directions, length, time, grading criteria, etc.—spelled out before starting?

need to understand the purpose of a task to approach it effectively?

learn better at certain times of the day?

You might find it interesting to apply these questions to yourself as well. Children sometimes learn styles of learning from their parents.

Computers in the Classroom

The computer—or more precisely, the microcomputer—has emerged in recent years as a viable and valuable teaching tool. It is particularly well suited to special education instruction and promises to enhance dramatically the efforts of special educators. While the computer cannot replace a teacher (computers still cannot convey sensitivity, compassion, warmth, or enthusiasm), it embodies many of the characteristics of an effective special educator: it gives a student undivided attention; it can motivate even the most disaffected youngster; it can individualize the instruction in accordance with a student's skill level, work pace, and learning style; it can teach a skill in sequential steps; it has infinite patience and can repeat a task or question endlessly; for most children it is nonthreatening, and it is nonjudgmental; it provides continuous and immediate feedback and minimizes failure and frustration; and it can measure the student's progress and identify areas of mastery and nonmastery. Special educators are increasingly recognizing and tapping this potential. Almost one-fourth of the microcomputers in school today are used in special education programs.

Special educators have yet to realize the computer's full potential, in part because available software (that is, the computer programs) geared to students with disabilities is limited, and many available programs are poorly designed. But many are using it with students who have a broad spectrum of learning problems and for a variety of purposes. Here are some examples:

A student with a reading problem can receive multisensory instruction that reinforces word-decoding skills through auditory and visual feedback.

A student who has trouble remembering math facts can use a computer program to practice multiplication facts.

A student with a handwriting problem can compose assignments on a word processor without the frustrations of writing and with the assurance of legibility.

A student with problems in oral communication can type a message into a computer, and a speech synthesizer can transform it into speech. Speech synthesizers can also enable students with visual impairments to hear printed material.

A student whose arm and hand movements are restricted can perform academic tasks on a computer using such devices as a joystick or a light pen.

A student with a high activity level and an impulsive approach to academic tasks can use a computer to learn to reflect before responding.

A student with a history of school failure and low self-esteem can derive confidence from using computer programs that ensure academic success.

A student receiving instruction in a home or hospital setting can communicate by computer with a teacher at school by using a device called a "modem" to hook up a school and home computer.

Microcomputers clearly have a place in special education. What is less clear is whether schools are using them effectively. How can you ensure that its potential is tapped? The first step is to find out whether your district is using computers, and if so, how. Your child, the principal, the director of special education or special services, the coordinator of the school district's computer program, or a science or mathematics teacher may provide answers to such questions as these: Is the school district using computers in the classroom? Are they being used in the special education program? How many? How often? For what purposes? Are teachers trained in their use? Are the software programs appropriate for your child's learning activities and special needs?

In general, you can assume that if your child's school has introduced microcomputers into the classroom, your youngster should not be excluded from using them on the basis of an educational disability. Furthermore, your child should not be using a microcomputer only for practice and drill; programs that enhance cognitive skills can be used effectively with special education students. If you believe that the district's computer program is inadequate, you may want to take the lead in exploring, through appropriate school channels, how it can be upgraded. In this advocacy effort, you may want to speak with other parents and consult professionals who have expertise in the application of computers to the schools.

If you have a computer at home, you can also use it as a learning tool with your child; it can also make homework less of a chore. While many educational programs are commercially available, they vary widely in quality and in appropriateness for students with special needs. In addition, not all software programs work on all computers—an important point to remember if you are shopping for a computer. If you are considering buying a home computer, talk to the teacher or another school staff member to find out what programs are most likely to help your youngster now and over the next several years, and which ones are consistent with the school's instructional approach; then look at the machines that can run those programs.

Behavior Modification

Teachers of special education students frequently use the principles and techniques of behavior modification to improve academic skills and classroom behavior. Behavior modification is the systematic application of the tenets of learning theory to change behavior. Behavior modification programs try to reduce or eliminate altogether an undesirable form of behavior and replace it with more desirable behavior by modifying events that precede or follow the behavior. You have undoubtedly used behavior modification techniques many times without realizing it: have you ever said your daughter could have dessert if she finished her vegetables? or that your son would have to forego watching television on school nights if he didn't get his homework done?

Teachers have long made use of behavior modification: in the twelfth century, Jewish students were promised figs, nuts, and honey if they mastered their Torah lessons. Behavior modification programs can take a variety of forms in educational settings. A teacher's smile or praise, a sticker on an excellent paper, detention, report card grades, and peer reaction to a student's behavior all are examples of behavior modification at work. Teachers may apply these principles in a systematic way to deal with a variety of classroom problems such as erratic attendance, wandering attention, incomplete assignments, disruptive outbursts, failure to master math facts, or talking out of turn. The program used with your child may be quite simple—for example, the teacher can consistently praise desired behavior and ignore undesired behavior, or allow your youngster to play games once seatwork is finished. Or, they can be more complex—for example, rewarding specific behavior with points that can be exchanged for privileges or material rewards. Behavior modification programs have proven particularly effective in helping children with severe disabilities to develop new skills and behavior.

It is a matter of incentive—little different in concept from using a potential pay raise or promotion to spur job performance. When a teacher offers rewards as an incentive, the goal is always to move away from the tangible reward and toward intrinsic satisfaction as the reinforcement for the behavior. While it is preferable to modify behavior through positive reinforcement, inappropriate behavior can also be discouraged through consequences that your child will probably seek to avoid—for example, loss of attention or privileges, detention, or loss of points. Whatever form the program takes, it should be systematically developed, consistently applied, and carefully monitored to achieve optimal results. And, it must be used with caution. If your child's special education program uses behavior modification, make sure that this technique has been introduced for your child's benefit rather than for the school's convenience.

How can you be sure of this? The first step is to look back at the IEP to see whether behavior modification has been called for, and to review the goals and objectives it is intended to further. If it has not been included, this is the starting point of a constructive conversation with the classroom teacher or school psychologist. If it has been included, you might ask the teacher to clarify how the behavior modification strategies are helping your child move toward a particular goal.

You can join forces with your child's teacher to develop and implement a behavior modification program. In fact, a program that is in effect both at home and in school is often more helpful. The keys to this partnership are a clear understanding of the program's purposes and procedures and frequent communication between you and the teacher to monitor your youngster's progress. How would it work? If your child were consistently not completing seatwork assigned in class, for example, you and the teacher might agree on a program of positive reinforcement. The teacher would let you know on a daily or weekly basis how your youngster was doing in this area; you could respond to positive performance by providing the incentives that you deem most appropriate (such as praise, special privileges, material rewards, or points) according to prearranged criteria. The daily report card (see Figure 5.3) is an example of a communication system that parents and teachers can use.

Learning About Feelings

Schools have traditionally interpreted their primary mandate as imparting academic skills, but many educators also stress affective education, which aims to help students understand and deal with their own and others' feelings, and to get along cooperatively with others. The increasing emphasis placed on this area by many teachers reflects a growing conviction that promoting emotional and social growth is not only a means to a desired end—improved academic performance—but also a worthy goal in its own right. Most special educators need little persuasion of its importance. They witness first-hand every day the intertwining of educational performance and social and emotional adjustment. Their learning problems may impede development of appropriate social skills; for example, a learning-disabled child may have difficulty in accurately "reading" other children's facial expressions or gestures. Special education students are particularly vulnerable to feelings of low self-esteem as a result of academic failure and teasing or outright rejection by their schoolmates. Your child's feelings of inadequacy can block academic progress as much as any other learning problem that shows up in the evaluation process.

Affective education is not psychoanalysis or group therapy; most special education teachers are not licensed to deliver that kind of service, and would not do so in school even if they were. But affective education can help youngsters to

identify and understand their own feelings and those of others;
express feelings and thoughts in an appropriate and assertive way;
realistically take stock of their own strengths and weaknesses;
understand their own values, needs, and goals, and examine the
    consequences of their choices;
develop self-esteem and confidence;
interact with others appropriately and resolve social conflicts ef-
    fectively;

understand and respect differences among individuals and among groups.

While special educators may use formal programs of affective education in their classrooms, this kind of instruction cannot really be separated from the teacher's personal classroom style. Most teachers engage in affective education throughout the school day through their actions and statements, the classroom climate they provide, and the relationships they develop with their students. In this way, teachers often hold powerful sway over their students and can leave lasting imprints on children's self-concepts. They can also shape students' social interactions through the models they provide in the classroom.

SPECIAL EDUCATION IN THE SECONDARY SCHOOL

For many (but certainly not all) special education students, the instruction they receive in secondary school (usually grades six or seven through twelve) is their last formal educational experience. Special education at the secondary level assumes a vital role in preparing these students for the vocational, consumer, and interpersonal challenges they face when they leave school.

The transition from elementary to secondary school is among the most difficult school adjustments that any child faces, and particularly a student with special needs. Your child is probably leaving a small, relatively uncomplicated educational setting with student-oriented teachers and easy-to-master rules and routines, and entering a larger, more complex setting with content-oriented teachers and a confusing array of regulations and procedures. Since youngsters with disabilities often have difficulty adapting to change, your child may find the transition overwhelming. This section aims to help you understand some of these secondary school roadblocks so you can help your child prepare for and cope with them. Your first step is to get a handle on the new school and its potential pitfalls (as well as its resources) for students with special needs.

Adjusting to the New School

Secondary schools are often large, labyrinthine buildings that accommodate great numbers of students. The size and complexity may confuse and intimidate your youngster, and its lack of intimacy may lessen his or her sense of involvement and belonging. Your child may, like many other new entrants into the school, be afraid of getting lost. If your youngster has difficulty with spatial relations or is used to a much smaller building, this concern may be justifiable. You might want to relieve your child's anxiety and ease the adjustment by asking to take your child on a tour of the new school before the first classes are held. (Many districts conduct orientation tours for new students as a matter of course.)

The school day in secondary schools is usually divided into several class periods, with your child moving from one class to another and from one teacher to another. Most students experience some apprehension as they adjust to the schedule and to navigating around school; these first few days may be more traumatic for students with disabilities. They may struggle to master the different routines and expectations of as many as six or seven teachers, as well as the school's rules and procedures. Such seemingly simple tasks as opening a combination locker or reading a schedule (often a computer printout) may prove bewildering. Your youngster may not only be confused by these varying demands, but also lack the confidence and assertiveness to seek out help from a homeroom teacher or guidance counselor.

Secondary teachers typically receive different training and use different teaching strategies than elementary teachers. Regular secondary teachers are usually trained in the teaching of specific subjects (such as science or history) and have generally had limited exposure to students with disabilities, the teaching of reading, or individualized teaching strategies. Because they typically see between 125 and 150 students each day, secondary teachers are often more geared to their content areas and to the needs of their classes as groups than to the needs of individual youngsters. They may teach by lecturing and are less likely than elementary-level or special education teachers to individualize instruction, monitor a student's grasp of instructions, provide detailed feedback, or offer suggestions aimed at a particular student. Regular classroom instruction at the secondary level therefore places a premium on such skills as listening, memory, note-taking, organization, test-taking, and independence, troublesome areas for many students with disabilities.

Should you be filling in, providing the one-on-one help that a regular secondary school teacher may not have the time to offer? This depends, of course, on your youngster's needs. In any case, you may need to walk a fine line between helping to organize and structure your child's schoolwork and encouraging your child to assume responsibility for these tasks.

The regular academic curriculum in secondary schools typically includes courses in English, mathematics, science, and history as well as a selection of elective classes. The focus is on imparting information rather than teaching academic skills. Course requirements and curricula may be designed by curriculum specialists who know a great deal about the content area, but much less about the educational needs of students with disabilities. As a result, the curriculum objectives for a particular course may not necessarily reflect the needs of your youngster. In helping to assemble your child's secondary program, you therefore need to weigh the value of your youngster's participation in a mainstream class against the value of a more segregated, but also more individualized, special education class.

Educational Approaches

Secondary students may receive special education in the full range of placements discussed in chapter 4 (see figure 4.2). Many attend resource rooms in which they may receive direct instruction in a particular subject, tutoring to help them through a mainstream class, or assistance in developing effective learning and study skills. Students who require much more intensive specialized instruction may attend a special class, either in a regular or special school. Many school districts have tried to lessen the stigma of special classes in regular schools by arranging for students with special needs to switch classes and teachers in the same manner as other students without lessening the amount or the intensity of special education. An important and growing practice is to provide instruction in community-based settings (for example, at job sites) to ease the student's transition from school to the community.

Since secondary school may be a youngster's last experience with formal education, secondary special educators need to adopt a broader focus than just imparting basic academic skills. The needs of their students may require that they also provide instruction in vocational, daily-living, and social skills. As part of the IEP team, you have an opportunity to help plan your youngster's secondary program, so you need to consider what skills your daughter or son might need for vocational success and personal satisfaction after leaving school and suggest that they be covered in the IEP.

Secondary special educators employ a range of educational approaches to meet their students' diverse needs. Your youngster's program will probably incorporate some of the strategies described below.

Remedial Approach. Special educators most frequently use the remedial approach at the secondary level. Teachers using this approach provide instruction in basic academic skills (reading, language arts, and mathematics). Using specialized materials at your youngster's instructional level, the teacher attempts to narrow the gap between actual and expected skills levels. This approach aims at helping your child make a successful transition to the regular education program. For many students, teachers aim for a minimum of a sixth- or seventh-grade reading level, which will boost their chances for achieving in mainstream classes and provide them with the minimal tools to meet the reading demands of the everyday world.

If your son's or daughter's basic academic skills are weak due to a history of inadequate or inappropriate instruction, the remedial approach may hasten progress. But if your child's basic skills are extremely tenuous despite consistently adequate schooling, remedial instruction at the secondary level is unlikely to raise your child's skills to the level of those of most other students at the same grade level. At this point, you might more realistically expect modest academic gains. Many students who receive remedial instruction reach a plateau in their basic skills at about their sophomore year in high school, after which they make little progress. If you, your child, or a teacher notice this plateau effect, you will want to be sure that the remedial approach gives way to other educational strategies that may be more beneficial.

Tutorial Approach. The special educator may provide instruction in content areas such as social studies or science to help your student keep pace with the regular curriculum. The teacher may instruct a small group of special education students in the same subject matter taught in the mainstream class but may introduce materials and teaching methods geared to the students' learning styles. This approach allows special education students to absorb the same information as their grademates at a level that promises comprehension and success. An alternative tutorial approach is to have a special education student attend a mainstream content-area class while receiving supportive instruction in that subject in a resource room.

Learning Strategies Approach. The learning strategies approach involves teaching your youngster new ways of acquiring, retaining, and communicating information—in short, new ways of learning. The general intent is to teach students how to learn more effectively; the specific aim is to provide them with tools that will help them achieve in mainstream classes. Your youngster might therefore be taught such skills as taking part in class discussions, following directions, taking notes, using textbooks, skimming, studying for tests, taking tests, budgeting time, proofreading, using the library, using various reference materials, and setting priorities. This approach is most effective when these thinking and learning skills are taught in the context of specific class assignments.

Functional Approach.   Depending on the nature of your youngster's disability, he or she may need formal instruction in skills needed to function effectively in the everyday world. For some, this may mean instruction in specific functional skills to complement an otherwise academically oriented program; for others, those with more severe disabilities, this may mean the use of a primarily functional curriculum in a self-contained class or community-based setting that stresses the teaching of self-care, social, community-involvement, consumer, vocational, and home-management skills. In a program with a functional emphasis, your youngster might learn, for example, how to read a want ad, complete a job application, understand an instuction manual, manage money, care for clothes, obtain a driver's license, register to vote, or read a map. A student who has only minimal reading skills might be taught to read such words as *exit, yield, stop, fire, danger, application, signature, sale,* and *credit*. You can help identify areas of instruction from which your son or daughter might profit based on your own observations of your youngster and discussions of post–high school goals.

Vocational Education

Like many other parents of special education students, you may have concerns about your youngster's adjustment to leaving school. In many cases, these concerns are well founded. Young people who have disabilities have often fared poorly after leaving school. A disproportionate number are unsuccessful in negotiating the transition between the classroom and the workplace: many cannot find employment; those who do often work at low-paying jobs beneath their ability.

Recent statistics show that most people who have disabilities received no systematic program of vocational education while in high school, and consequently left school without entry-level job skills. In the past, vocational training was provided to select groups of special education students, such as the mentally retarded, and was limited to lower-level skill training. Studies have shown, however, that people

138

with severe disabilities are able to perform complex tasks with appropriate training. For example, moderately and severely retarded adults in a University of Oregon program were taught to put together a fifty-two-piece cam switch assembly. The employment problems experienced by people with disabilities apparently stem less from their limitations than from inadequate training—and, of course, employers' lack of exposure to the abilities of people who have disabilities.

Recognizing the problems faced by this sector of the workforce, Congress passed four landmark legislative acts:

- Section 504 of the Rehabilitation Act of 1973 forbids discrimination against the handicapped by federally supported agencies and requires vocational training opportunities for handicapped students comparable to those provided for the general student population.
- Public Law 94–142 requires that schools provide vocational education to special education students if deemed appropriate by the IEP team. The program must be specially designed, if necessary, to meet the student's educational needs. These vocational programs must be provided in the least restrictive environment.
- Public Law 94–482 requires that states earmark 10 percent of their federal vocational funds for the vocational training of handicapped students.
- Public Law 98–524 requires that school districts (1) inform parents of special education students about its vocational education programs and eligibility requirements by no later than the beginning of ninth grade; (2) evaluate the interests, abilities, and special needs of all students with disabilities who enroll in vocational programs; (3) offer specialized educational services, including modification of curriculum, instruction, equipment, and facilities necessary for students with special needs to learn effectively; and (4) provide career development activities and counseling services to facilitate the transition from school to the working world.

School districts have responded to this legislative impetus with an increasing number of vocational programs. These programs can assume a wide variety of forms, so you need to be sure that you understand the full range of vocational options offered by your school district. Your youngster may receive vocational training in a regular vocational program or in a program restricted to students with disabilities. (The more appropriate placement for a student who has a mild learning disability is usually the regular program.) Programs may run as short as one year or as long as four. A student in a vocational program may receive on-the-job experience by working at an actual employment site or in a simulated work setting.

If a vocational education program is specially designed to meet your youngster's needs, it must be written into the IEP. This means that you have an opportunity to take part in its development. Below are some basic principles and practices that you might keep in mind during that process.

- *Make sure that academic and vocational goals* that promote your child's postschool adjustment are included in the IEP and that the educational services are appropriate to reaching these goals.
- *The development of appropriate vocational programs* requires comprehensive and ongoing assessment of your child's interests, abilities, and disabilities to enable the IEP team and the teachers to make the best possible match between your youngster's characteristics and the program.
- *Vocational programs for students with special needs* are often most effective when they reflect the cooperative efforts of the vocational and special educator. You might request that both attend the IEP meeting.
- *The vocational program must take place* in the least restrictive environment. If your youngster can learn effectively in a regular vocational program, he or she must be placed there. The school district must provide supportive services and instructional aids if that is what it takes for your son or daughter to benefit from the program.
- *Vocational education programs should include* instruction in not only the technical skills associated with a specific job, but also the competencies required to obtain and maintain employment (for example, filling out applications, writing a resumé, responding to interview questions, and selecting appropriate clothing).
- *The school should make efforts to place your daughter or son* in the community, where newly learned skills can be practiced at actual work sites. This community mainstreaming effort should ideally include job placement counseling upon leaving school. If necessary, arrangements should be made for your youngster to

receive services from the state vocational rehabilitation agency, which generally provides employment services to people with disabilities.

• *It is important to balance* the vocational instruction with academic instruction to ensure that your daughter or son leaves school with a base of skills that allows effective functioning in the everyday world.

Graduation

The school district must give your youngster the opportunity to earn a high school diploma, no matter how severe his or her disability. The automatic exclusion of a student from educational programs leading to graduation would violate Section 504, the federal antidiscrimination law.

The establishment of graduation standards that take into account the educational status of students with disabilities has been complicated by the minimum competency testing movement that took hold in the mid-1970s. In an attempt to raise the academic achievement of its high school graduates, many states have enacted legislation requiring that students achieve a minimum level on tests of reading, writing, and mathematics before they can graduate. States have applied this requirement to students with disabilities in different ways: some require all students, including special education students, to pass the minimum competency test to graduate; others allow special education students to be exempted from the requirement.

The graduation process for your daughter or son is primarily a state-regulated practice and is governed by state and local guidelines. States have developed diverse approaches to the awarding of high school diplomas to students with disabilities. The following paragraphs describe the most common approaches.

The ''one-diploma, same-requirements'' approach awards the same diploma to all students—with or without disabilities—who meet a single set of requirements. (In some school districts, special education classes do not count toward graduation.) While this approach avoids the stigma of a special education or nonstandard diploma, it can result in the denial of diplomas to students who do not pass all the required courses, who do not receive credit for special education classes, or who do not pass the minimum competency test. If this approach is used, testing and instructional modifications (for example, presenting the minimum competency test in braille or large print, or extending the time a special education student can stay in school) are essential to allowing special education students to meet graduation requirements. If these modifications are not permitted, the school district may be violating Section 504—if it can be shown that your youngster is denied a diploma solely because of his or her disability.

The "one-diploma, flexible-requirements" approach makes all students eligible for the same diploma, although special education students may be held to graduation requirements based on their learning characteristics. These requirements are determined by the IEP team on an individual basis: Barbara, who attends mainstream classes but receives support in a resource room, might be required to meet the same criteria set for regular education classmates, including passing the minimum competency test; Michael, who receives instruction primarily in special education classes, might be required to meet all of the goals and objectives stated in his IEP, and might be exempted from the minimum competency test requirement. If this is the approach your school district takes, you can help to develop these graduation criteria at an IEP meeting.

The "two-diploma" approach makes all students eligible to receive the standard diploma upon meeting the prescribed graduation requirements. Special education students who fail to meet these requirements but meet the criteria specified in the IEP would qualify to graduate and receive a nonstandard diploma. This diploma might differ from the standard diploma, for example, by its designation as a "special education" diploma, and by a statement that the student has qualified to graduate by meeting all the IEP requirements. This approach allows your youngster to graduate and receive a diploma without necessarily meeting the same standards required of schoolmates who do not have disabilities; on the other hand, it may increase the stigma attached to special education, lessening the value of your youngster's educational experience and fostering job discrimination.

The "certificate of attendance or completion" approach awards a certificate of completion to special education students who finish a prescribed course of study but fail to meet the graduation requirements. This certificate does not, however, represent graduation from high school, and may be unfair to students who are unable to meet graduation requirements by virtue of a disability.

Whatever approach is used will probably prove problematic in practice, and provoke some claims of unfairness. Any approach that draws a line between groups of students is likely to be unfair to those who fall close to the line, especially since it is difficult to reliably differentiate between students who have an educational disability and students who do not.

IS COLLEGE IN YOUR CHILD'S FUTURE?

The exhilaration of graduation may quickly turn to apprehension as your youngster ponders the decisions and experiences that lie ahead. June may mean entry into the job market, or enrollment in a vocational training program. For some special education students—those with average or above-average intelligence, good conceptual ability, a high level of academic motivation, and a willingness to work diligently to compensate for learning problems—college may be a viable postgraduation option. Does your son or daughter have these characteristics? If not, college may mean only failure and frustration.

The college planning process for your youngster must start early. The sophomore year of high school is not too soon to begin gathering information, reviewing applications, and finding out what course and testing requirements must be fulfilled. Your youngster may take the Scholastic Aptitude Test or the American College Testing assessment in a nonstandardized manner to minimize the effect of a disability on test performance. The SAT is available in large type, braille, and on audiocassette, and can be administered in an extended time frame or with the assistance of a reader. If one or more of these modifications is made, the resulting score is reported to colleges with the notation "nonstandard administration." When you and your youngster decide whether to request a modification of the testing procedures, balance the advantage of a test score that reflects actual ability against the disadvantage of the "nonstandard administration" notation, which may in the minds of some admissions officers raise doubts about the legitimacy of the score. Whatever decision you make, keep in mind that admissions officers are not likely to place great weight on test scores of applicants who have a special education background. They probably would place more weight on teacher recommendations and the personal interview.

The college selection process requires painstaking research. You can obtain information by consulting college guides (see *For Further Information* at the end of the chapter); talking with knowledgeable persons (such as guidance counselors, special education professionals, private educational counselors, and other parents who have experienced similar circumstances); and writing to colleges for their free literature. The search may include colleges with specific programs for learning-disabled students, as well as two- and four-year colleges that do not offer formal programs but welcome students with special needs and offer supportive services.

While a number of colleges across the country offer formal programs for the learning-disabled, the quality of the programs and the services offered vary widely. You and your youngster must look beyond the brochures touting the program to obtain specific information, such as:

- What are the entrance requirements? (Some colleges have the same requirements for students with and without disabilities; other colleges have more flexible admissions standards for students with disabilities.) What tests are required for admission?
- Does the college have a separate program for students with special needs, with advisers trained to work with them? Or does the college only offer support services without a separate program coordinator and staff?
- Is your youngster eligible for or required to participate in any special programs or courses? (Some colleges require summer courses in study skills or a commitment to counseling as a condition of admission.) Does your youngster receive credits toward graduation for summer courses?
- What services are available to your youngster? (Examples of services or learning aids include: diagnostic testing, learning labs, IEPs developed for individual students, taped books, note takers, readers, sign-language interpreters, individual and group counseling, print enlargers, calculators, reading machines, computer labs equipped with hardware and software geared to students with disabilities.)
- What remedial and tutoring services are available? What is the ratio of remedial instructor or tutor to students? What are the backgrounds of the tutors?
- What accommodations do faculty make in teaching students with disabilities? (These may include allowing students to tape lectures, take untimed exams, take oral instead of written exams, or submit tape recordings instead of written papers.)
- Can your student take a reduced course load or waive or substitute for required courses?
- What percentage of the college's student population is disabled? What is the record of students with disabilities who have attended the college? To what degree have they been able to participate in the college's activities? What is their attrition rate?
- Will the college transcript contain such notations as ''special admission''? (It is preferable that it does not.)

To answer these and other questions, take a tour of the college with your son or daughter, talk with its staff, and ask the admissions office to refer you to past or present students who have disabilities (and their parents).

For a student who has special needs and wants to attend college, mastering a range of learning skills may spell the difference between failure and success. (These skills are critical for all college students.) They include: note-taking, studying for tests, test-taking, typing, using textbooks, underlining, skimming, using the library, writing research papers, budgeting time, making and remembering appointments, getting to class on time, and asserting oneself in a range of situations. If a disability impedes these skills, your youngster will need to develop compensating strategies or take advantage of supportive services. Slow or disabled readers can listen to books on tape. Recording for the Blind, Inc. (20 Roszel Rd., Princeton, N.J. 08540) makes available books or tapes at no cost to students who are blind, or who have a visual impairment, or a physical or perceptual disability. Its library of recorded books includes more than 60,000 titles, and if necessary it will record books which are not yet taped. Some private schools, such as the Landmark School in Massachusetts, offer programs to develop academic and study skills for post-high school students planning to enter college. The college your youngster attends may also offer a summer program prior to the first year.

Even with this advance preparation and the development of compensating strategies, students with disabilities must recognize that they will have to work longer and harder than most of their classmates to achieve on a par with them. College instructors are not likely to adapt their academic standards for students with disabilities; on the other hand, they are forbidden by Section 504 to discriminate against a student because of a handicap. For example, a blind student must be provided with alternate methods to receive information.

Before the first semester begins, you may want to join your youngster in a discussion with the dean of students, the student adviser, and the instructors to inform them of any special circumstances that may require accommodation and to find out what services are available and how they can be obtained. Upper-class students can also provide helpful information.

SPECIAL ISSUES IN SPECIAL EDUCATION

Grades

Grades are intended to inform you and your child about his or her achievement, progress, and effort. A simple letter or number cannot adequately convey all these aspects of performance, so special education teachers usually must decide which aspect to weigh most heavily in assigning a grade. This dilemma is also faced by regular education teachers: should they grade students with disabilities according to their achievement level relative to their classmates, or according to their rate of improvement in relation to their own past performance, or according to their effort and attitude, or a combination of these factors? Grades should reflect, to some extent, your youngster's progress and effort. These are examples of grading systems used with special education students:

> checklist of skills/concepts mastered;
> narrative comments by the teacher;
> letter or number grades supplemented by the teacher's narrative comments;
> letter grades based on degree of completion of predetermined objectives (which may be coordinated with the IEP); or
> letter grades to reflect student's progress and effort with a number notation indicating actual level of functioning.

Whatever grading system is used, it should be as close as possible in format and procedure to that used with regular education students to lessen the stigma of the special education experience.

Because of the different formats and criteria used by districts and teachers to rate the performance of special education students, you may not be clear about the meaning of the grades your child brings home. In this case, do not hesitate to contact the teacher to get clarification.

Homework

Mention the word *homework* to children who have learning problems and their anxiety may skyrocket; mention the same word to their parents and a similar reaction is probable. Homework, in this book, means any task done at home that is related to the goals listed on the IEP. It may mean learning new vocabulary words or writing a research report. It may mean balancing a checkbook or practicing shoe-tying. It may mean taking part in a family discussion without interrupting.

You may have witnessed your youngster's exasperation as he or she tries to complete assignments or carry out tasks that are too long, too confusing, or too hard. For many parents, this situation poses dilemmas. How insistent should you be that the assignment must be finished? How can you tell if the work really is "too hard"?

The issue of homework does not fade when your child enters a special education program; there may be homework assigned in the special education or regular education classes that your youngster attends. The assignments your child brings home are likely to be tailored to his or her learning characteristics, but your youngster may still want or need your help. Should you help? Some teachers say yes, while others, concerned that you might confuse, frustrate, or discourage your child, prefer that you "leave the teaching to the teachers." Both viewpoints have merit. Numerous studies show that parents can provide valuable academic support to their children as long as it remains on a positive, relatively tension-free level. But you need to monitor your own reactions: when you find yourself becoming frustrated, impatient, or irritable—as all homework-helping parents occasionally do—you are undoubtedly conveying these feelings to your youngster and it is time to stop. Continuing despite this tension will have little educational value and may dishearten your child. If assistance is needed and you cannot work calmly with your child—as many otherwise patient parents cannot—hire a tutor, if this is economically feasible, or work out an exchange with another parent in a similar situation. Sometimes parents can work with other children more easily than with their own.

You may find the following suggestions useful in working with your son or daughter. (These suggestions may not be suitable for all students with disabilities. Use your own good judgment and follow those that make sense in light of your youngster's learning characteristics.)

- Keep in mind that the goal is to foster independence and self-confidence in completing an assigned task. Give suggestions and support, but don't do the task for your child.
- Provide a setting conducive to work. While this is usually a quiet, well-lit area free of distraction, some children may work better with background noise such as music.
- Choose a time when your child is alert and responsive.
- Don't interfere with a favorite activity (yours or your child's) such as a special TV show. That only heightens inattention and impatience.
- Encourage good homework habits, including (when appropriate) writing the assignment down, bringing the proper materials home, and bringing homework back to school. If necessary, ask the teacher to write down the assigned task on the blackboard or a piece of paper.

• If your child doesn't understand the task, offer an explanation that is compatible with the teacher's explanation. Do the first problem or question as a model and let your child do the others, providing only as much guidance as needed.

• If a reading assignment is accompanied by questions your child needs to answer, review the questions together before he or she reads the passage.

• Begin with relatively easy tasks to generate confidence and gradually move to the more difficult tasks.

• Comment positively on your child's successes and good efforts and avoid negative or disparaging comments when your youngster experiences difficulty.

• Determine the optimal length of the work session, which will vary with the child and the nature of the task, and try not to exceed it.

• If the assignments are too long or too hard (or not sufficiently challenging), talk with the teacher about making a change.

• If the homework is not a paper-and-pencil assignment (practice in self-grooming, for example, or practice in pronouncing certain sounds), you might want to write a note telling the teacher how your youngster fared with the task.

School Discipline

Like all other students, those in special education are subject to disciplinary measures at school. However, federal law prohibits the school from disciplining a student for behavior resulting from a disability. To do so would violate Section 504 by discriminating against a person with a disability.

What may seem crystal clear in theory can be quite murky in practice. Emily, a fifth grader whose communication difficulties often cause frustration, has just pushed Robert down the steps of the school bus. How does a responsible school official decide whether the incident stemmed from Emily's disability? The answer is, not easily. And, experience has shown, not consistently. School districts apply varying standards in disciplining or not disciplining special education students. Some districts have developed a range of alternative procedures to use when these youngsters exhibit behavior problems; others hold special education students to the same disciplinary standards applied to the school's general student population, despite the Section 504 mandate.

If you anticipate that your youngster may have behavior problems in school, you might discuss strategies for dealing with those problems which are sensitive to your child's needs. The IEP meeting is an appropriate time to discuss these issues. In fact, the IEP team can write into the IEP specific procedures to be used when your youngster acts out. If this aspect of your child's schooling was not discussed at the IEP meeting, it is not too late to speak up. Arrange a meeting with the school administrator responsible for discipline to discuss alternative procedures to be used with your child, or ask that a new IEP meeting be called so that the IEP can be amended to include behavioral issues. The following are examples of alternative courses of action you might propose for inclusion in the IEP:

- notification of the parents by the school if the child exhibits behavior problems
- development of a systematic behavior modification program with rewards or special privileges for appropriate behavior and loss of privileges for inappropriate behavior
- removal of a student to a quiet place such as a carrel, a corner of the room, or a separate room where he or she can "cool down"
- immediate access to a specified school staff member with whom the student has rapport to discuss and try to resolve the problem
- providing peer feedback to the student
- regular counseling by a school staff member like a guidance counselor, school psychologist, or social worker
- preventive measures such as a class meeting to set rules and consequences, role playing, alternative educational approaches (for example, "hands-on" activities or independent projects), and avoidance of troublesome activities or peer combinations

A few words about suspension and expulsion. As a general rule, school districts may suspend students from school for serious violations of school rules; out-of-school suspensions are not intended to be used for isolated minor infractions. Expulsion, or the permanent exclusion from school, is to be used only when no other course of action is appropriate. There is a restriction on the use of suspensions and expulsions for students with disabilities, namely the requirement that the due-process procedures outlined in Public Law 94–142 (which guarantees your right to review records, receive written notice of the school's proposed action, and challenge the action) be followed before a change in educational placement takes place. A long-term suspension (generally for more than ten days) or an expulsion is considered a change in educational placement, which requires a meeting of the IEP team to revise the educational program if necessary, and entitles parents to invoke the above procedures, including a due-process hearing. This principle does not, however, prohibit the school district from removing a student from a classroom where he or she is endangering others or significantly disrupting a class. In any case, if the school district expels a special education student from a public school setting, it must still offer him or her a free appropriate public education in an alternative setting.

Medication

Your child may receive medication for problems related to his or her disability. (These medications must be prescribed by a licensed physician.) For example, elementary school children with high activity levels and short attention spans may be prescribed such medications as Ritalin or Cylert; although these medications act as stimulants when they are given to adults, they may have a calming effect on "hyperactive" children, making them more receptive to instruction. A learning problem in and of itself, however, does not indicate a need for medication.

The use of stimulant medication for these purposes is controversial. While a discussion of the pros and cons is beyond the scope of this book, at a minimum you might want to explore with your doctor the wisdom of giving your child such medication or alternative forms of intervention. Keep in mind that the medication does not remediate the learning problem, but it may enhance your child's ability to absorb instruction. Medication does not teach—people do.

If you agree that your youngster needs medication, it may need to be administered in school. In this case, be sure to ask about the district's policies and procedures. The school district must have your consent, and that of a physician, to administer medication in school. Medication is usually given by the school nurse, although in some schools a teacher or secretary assumes this responsibility. School officials will probably ask for information from the prescribing physician about its purpose, how the medication should be administered, how often, and possible side effects. You should also be aware of this information. If you are not satisfied with the doctor's explanation, consult the *Physicians' Desk Reference* (PDR) in your local library.

Just as the school needs information from the doctor, so too the doctor needs information from the school to monitor the effectiveness of the medication. Two students may react differently to the same medication or the same dosage—the same pill may make one child sleepy and another restless. There is often a trial period during which the doctor varies the dosage to obtain the optimal effect. Your observations and those of the teacher are important in assessing the medication's positive or negative effects. Your youngster's behavior should be monitored beyond the initial trial period, however, since some medications lessen in their effect with time. Your feedback is also important when the medication is discontinued (as medication for "hyperactivity" usually is by the time your youngster reaches adolescence). Medication-free periods are essential: you might consider discontinuing the medication during the summer and at the start of the next school year to assess its efficacy. Communication among you, the doctor, and the teacher is essential to an effective and appropriate medication program. You might want to make certain that the prescribing physician is getting information about the effects of the medication at home and in school on a regular basis.

FOR FURTHER INFORMATION

Gadow, K. D. (1979). *Children on medication: A primer for school personnel.* Reston, Va.: Council for Exceptional Children. While intended primarily for educators, this research-based book may also help parents to understand the purposes and side effects of various medications prescribed for children.

Goldberg, K. P., and Sherwood, R. D. (1983). *Microcomputers—A parents' guide.* New York: John Wiley & Sons. A lucid and accessible introduction to microcomputers. Describes considerations in purchasing a microcomputer and their educational uses at home and in school, and offers a sampling of educational programs.

Hart, V. (1980). *Mainstreaming children with special needs.* New York: Longman. Provides practical information about a wide range of disabilities and their educational implications.

Marsh, G. E., Gearheart, C. K., and Gearheart, B. R. (1978). *The learning disabled adolescent—Program alternatives in the secondary school.* St. Louis: C. V. Mosby. A comprehensive discussion of the secondary student and setting.

Parents' Campaign for Handicapped Children (1983). *The life skills training: A program for parents and their learning-disabled teenagers.* Washington, D.C. A program designed to teach social and independent living skills. (See Appendix B for publisher's address.)

Patterson, G. R., and Gullion, M. E. (1976). *Living with children: New methods for parents and teachers.* Champaign, Ill.: Research Press. An easy-to-use guide to the principles of behavior modification as applied to a wide range of problems encountered at home and in school.

Pope, L. (1982). *Guidelines for teaching children with learning problems.* Brooklyn, N.Y.: Book-Lab. A handbook of teaching strategies and educational materials for use with students who have learning or behavioral problems.

The following guides describe postsecondary educational and training programs for students with disabilities.

Association for Children and Adults with Learning Disabilities. *List of colleges and universities that accept students with learning disabilities.* Pittsburgh, Pa.

Fielding, P. M. (1984). *A national directory of four year colleges, two year colleges, and post high school training programs for young people with learning disabilities*. Tulsa, Okla.: Partners in Publishing.

Liscio, M. A., ed. (1984). *A guide to colleges for learning disabled students*. Orlando, Fla.: Academic Press.

Mangrum, C. T., II, and Strichart, S. S. (1984). *College and the learning disabled student*. Orlando, Fla.: Grune and Stratton.

Ridenour, D. M., and Johnston, J. (1981). *A guide to post-secondary educational opportunities for the learning disabled*. Oak Park, Ill.: Time Out to Enjoy.

Skyer, R., and Skyer, G. (1982). *What do you do after high school?* Rockaway Park, N.Y.: Skyer Consultation Center.

The Educational Testing Service, which administers the Scholastic Aptitude Test, offers at no cost a pamphlet entitled *Information for students with special needs*. Write to: Educational Testing Service, Services for Handicapped Students, CN 6602, Princeton, N.J. 08541. For information about the American College Testing Program's special testing procedures, contact American College Testing Program, P.O. Box 168, Iowa City, Iowa 52243.

Closer Look/Parents' Campaign for Handicapped Children and Youth operates "LD Teenline," a national toll-free hotline providing information about learning disabilities among teens, and available educational and vocational programs. Parents can reach this service by calling 1-800-522-3458 from 10 a.m. to 4 p.m. (EST) Monday through Friday.

7

Resolving Conflicts with the School

During the course of the special education process, you and the school district may disagree about some aspect of your child's program. When this happens, the school's position does not necessarily prevail. In fact, Public Law 94–142 and Section 504 require that you have an opportunity to contest formally a school's recommendations or decisions. Similarly, school districts are entitled to challenge legally the decisions you make about your child's educational program (for example, if you refuse to consent to an initial placement in a special education program). The fact that you and school officials can take issue with each other's actions through a due-process hearing or other procedures helps ensure accountability at both ends and fosters compliance with the letter and spirit of the law.

You can pursue a number of avenues when you are in conflict with the school district. These are summarized below; the primary methods of conflict resolution are taken up in more detail later in this chapter.

- *Independent Educational Evaluation.* If you are dissatisfied with any aspect of the school's evaluation, you can request another evaluation by a team of professionals who are not affiliated with the school district. (See chapter 2.)
- *IEP Review.* If you think the IEP is no longer appropriate to your child's educational needs, you can request a meeting to review the IEP prior to the annual review date. (See chapter 4.)
- *Reevaluation.* If you believe your child is receiving an inappropriate educational program because of inaccurate or out-of-date information on his or her educational status, you may request a reevaluation before its scheduled time. (See chapter 1.)
- *Informal Meeting.* If you disagree with a school's action or recommendation, you can request to meet with the appropriate school officials to resolve the conflict. Some districts arrange for

153

an "administrative review," which is a formal mechanism for this school conference.

• *Mediation.* You and school officials may meet with a neutral third party to try to settle your differences.

• *Due-Process Hearing.* You or school officials can initiate a formal hearing before an impartial hearing officer who is empowered to resolve the dispute.

• *Formal Complaint.* Public Law 94–142 allows you to lodge a complaint with the state department of education if you believe the school is in violation of its legal obligations to your child. You can also contact the federal Office of Civil Rights if you believe a school district is violating Section 504 by discriminating against your child because of his or her disability.

CHALLENGING SCHOOL OFFICIALS

Settling a dispute with a school district often requires a confrontation, which does not come easily to many parents. You may be reluctant to disagree openly with school officials for many of the same reasons that you may be hesitant to assert your views at an IEP meeting (as discussed in chapter 5). In addition, you may worry that by challenging school officials, you might jeopardize your child's treatment at school. This is a possibility, of course, but it is more likely that once you are perceived as knowledgeable about your rights and special education and willing to challenge the school's actions, its staff will be especially careful to ensure that your child is receiving educational services that are appropriate and that comply fully with the IEP and the law.

Your disagreement with the school may not stem from inappropriate or bad-faith actions, but rather may result from differing priorities or constraints. As awkward and uncomfortable as it may be, conflict can prove beneficial by opening up lines of communication, and airing important issues. It gives you and the school district an opportunity to confront your differences honestly and openly, with or without a third party, to find a solution which is in your child's best educational interests. Your challenge may even give rise to new opportunities for your youngster and for other children with special needs. In several states, parents' willingness to take on the school system resulted in legal rulings that entitle some special education children to a twelve-month educational program.

The message is clear: do not hesitate to voice your disagreement with any school decision that in your view does not serve your young-ster's best educational interests.

Of course, there are risks involved; these risks need not deter you from your challenge, but you want to keep them in mind. Conflict may leave you and school officials embittered, jeopardizing your future working relationship and, in extreme cases, even the success of your child's educational program. In any conflict-resolution procedure, no matter what form it takes, your focus (and that of school officials) should be to deal with each other in good faith and with respect so that after the conflict is resolved, you can work cooperatively together on your child's behalf. The issue is not who wins or who loses, but rather what kind of educational program your child is to receive. This seems evident enough, but in the heat of argument it is easy enough to lose that focus.

INFORMAL CONFLICT RESOLUTION

When you have a disagreement with the school, your first step is to try to resolve it through informal, nonadversarial procedures. In short, ask to meet with the appropriate school officials. Resolving a problem informally is less likely to spark antagonism than a more for-mal, adversarial approach. It can also bring about a speedy resolution without cost to either party.

Make an appointment to see the person most closely connected with the issue that concerns you. For example, if you are troubled by your child's slow progress in reading, meet with the teacher. If you think a specific disciplinary measure is inappropriate for your child, meet with the principal. If the issue is the validity of specific test re-sults, make an appointment with the evaluator. If you take issue with the school district's interpretation of a state regulation, speak with the director of special education or special services. This meeting gives you a chance to gather information, to determine whether a problem does exist, and, if so, to work toward an acceptable solution. Solutions are most effective and carried out most quickly when they are developed jointly with the person who is actually responsible for its implemen-tation.

Of course, you may not be able to resolve the conflict at this level. You may be dissatisfied with a school official's response, or the in-dividual with whom you meet may lack the authority to effect the de-sired change. In this case, you need to speak with someone at the next higher rung in the school district's organizational ladder. If you already met with the teacher, the principal is your next step, and so on. Chapter 5 describes a hierarchy typical of many school districts, although the organization will vary somewhat with the district's size and administrative outlook.

If, as you work your way up the ladder, you still cannot resolve the issue, you might consider contacting the school superintendent (or, in a very large district, an assistant superintendent) either in a letter or by requesting a meeting. Or, you might bring the issue to the attention of the local board of education.

Dealing with your youngster's educational needs cannot be your full-time occupation, but it is time-consuming. Even at an informal meeting, solid preparation and an organized presentation can spell the difference between getting what you want and caving in when the professional on the other side of the desk makes a well-rehearsed case. Try to familiarize yourself with the appropriate special education practices in the areas of dispute and the applicable regulations. Other parents can be helpful here, as can parent advocates and special education associations. If necessary, consult a specialist. Although the meeting is informal, you can bring a guest with you to take notes, or serve as an adviser or spokesperson. You might also bring along any documents that support your position (for example, reports from an independent educational evaluation) and a summary of the steps you have taken at other levels to resolve the problem.

How you present your case may be crucial. You have your own style of speaking in these situations, but keep in mind that the best presentation is assertive and calm, and stays focused on specific issues and facts (and never on personalities). Personal attacks—no matter how justified your anger—only cloud the important issues and lessen the chance of an informal, speedy solution. Don't lose sight of your own goals, but do try to keep an open mind. Make an effort to understand the school district's rationale, acknowledge the school staff's good intentions when appropriate, and do consider alternative solutions if they do not compromise the quality of your child's program. The assertiveness strategies outlined in chapter 5 may be helpful to you at these informal meetings.

If you reach an agreement with the school district at this informal level, take the time to write a letter to the appropriate school official summarizing your understanding of the agreement and, in specific terms, the actions to be taken. Be sure to keep a copy for your records. If, on the other hand, you are still in conflict with the school district after exhausting this route, more formal avenues of challenge are now open to you.

MEDIATION

If the conflict is rooted in mistrust, miscommunication, or misinformation, mediation may prove an effective approach. This is a process for settling disputes through the intervention of an impartial third party. Although lacking authority to enforce a decision, the mediator tries to hammer out a settlement that is acceptable to both sides, serves your child's best interests, and complies with the law. Federal law encourages (but does not require) mediation, and it is gaining popularity as a method for resolving special education disputes between parents and schools. Some states now require that mediation be made available to you when you request a due-process hearing. If the mediation brings about a settlement, the hearing is not necessary; if it does not, the hearing can proceed.

Mediation offers advantages over the more formal, more adversarial due-process hearing. It is less costly in terms of time, emotional energy, and money, and it is less likely to engender animosity between you and school officials. Mediation provides an opportunity not only to resolve the problem amicably, but also establish lines of communication that may benefit your child in the future.

Success hinges on the willingness of all parties to engage actively and openly in a give-and-take process, and on the mediator's ability to bring about consensus. This is a time to put your confrontational posture in storage, so that you can listen effectively to the school official's position and concerns, and consider solutions that might not have occurred to you. At the same time, keep in mind that you are under no obligation to compromise during the mediation. Your decision to agree—or not to agree—rests only on your judgment of what is in your child's best interest (and not on what may be your natural desire to appear helpful and pleasant). If mediation is used by either party as a stalling tactic (to put off more formal proceedings), it is sure to fail.

Reaching a settlement at this stage may hinge on the mediator's skills. The ideal mediator is familiar with special education laws and practices, understands group dynamics, and takes a creative approach to problem solving. The bottom-line qualification is neutrality: he or she must have no professional or personal relationship with either party and must be perceived as unbiased. For this reason, a teacher or administrator from your school district would be an inappropriate mediator; so would your attorney or your pastor. Check with your district's director of special education or special services to find out procedures for obtaining a mediator; if the school cannot help you, contact the division of special education within the state department of education.

There are few ground rules. The mediator meets with you and school officials and encourages a calm, orderly discussion of substantive issues. You can bring a lawyer or advocate (as can the school district), but at this stage, direct communication may be better. The mediation session often takes place in a school district building, but if possible a neutral site (such as the mediator's own office) is preferable. The mediator attempts to build consensus by delineating areas of agreement and disagreement, helping each side to understand the merits of the other's position, providing information, clarifying misunderstandings or misconceptions, and offering alternative solutions. The mediator may want to meet privately with you (or the school officials) to help you to clarify your viewpoint and to encourage you to move in a particular direction based on the mediator's assessment of the strengths and weaknesses of your position. While the goal is to foster an agreement, a responsible mediator keeps in mind the child's interest and avoids pressuring either party to the point that it is intimidated into a settlement. The mediator must respect either party's right not to compromise, and must not accept an agreement that violates the law or your child's educational interests.

There are three possible outcomes: acceptance of one position over another; a compromise; or no agreement. If an agreement is reached, it must be put into writing and signed by both parties. If no agreement is reached, either party can request a hearing. (Letting the school know of your serious intention to request a formal—and often costly—due-process hearing can occasionally work wonders in securing a mediated settlement.)

THE DUE-PROCESS HEARING

This is a more formal, legalistic vehicle for conflict resolution. It is a legal proceeding in which an impartial hearing officer (or, in some states, a panel) hears your arguments and those of school officials. Witnesses may be called, evidence is presented, and a decision is rendered which is binding unless appealed. The purpose of the due-process hearing is to resolve a dispute involving an individual child, but its results can affect many other children by setting a precedent or providing clarification of controversial educational questions.

Hopefully, you have resolved your dispute by the time you get to this stage. Hearings are avenues of last resort, but you should not hesitate to request one if a genuine, substantial disagreement has not been resolved in any of the other available ways.

Basis for a Hearing

You can initiate a due-process hearing on any matter relating to the identification, evaluation, or educational placement of your child who has a disability (or a possible disability). Most hearings focus on whether an educational program is appropriate for a particular child, but you can request a hearing on a broad spectrum of issues. Here are some examples:

You think your child should be referred for evaluation and the school district does not.

You believe your child qualifies for special education and the school district, based on its evaluation, does not.

You think your child has been inaccurately classified as having a particular disability.

You think your child needs a self-contained special education setting, but the school district contends a resource room is the proper placement.

You believe that ethnic, cultural, or linguistic factors skewed the evaluation results.

You think your child requires a predominantly language-based special education program, and the school district disagrees.

You believe your child should be evaluated in his or her home language, and the school district disagrees.

You think that physical therapy should be provided as a related service, while the school district contends that the physical problem is not affecting your youngster's educational performance.

You think that your child needs a twelve-month educational program to prevent academic regression during the summer, and the school district argues that a 180-day program meets your child's educational needs.

You think your child needs five sessions per week of speech therapy, and the school district says that two sessions per week is adequate.

You place your child in a private school that meets his or her special needs, and you request tuition reimbursement from the school district; school officials refuse on the grounds that it can offer your son or daughter appropriate services in a public school setting.

You can initiate a hearing when you believe the school district is not meeting the obligations to your child specified in state or federal law. You cannot request a hearing, however, to review a question that lies within the school's discretion as long as the school is in compliance with the law. For example, you cannot request a hearing to challenge a school district's refusal to assign your child to a different teacher if the present teacher meets state qualifications.

Should You Request a Hearing?

Once you have exhausted the various informal approaches to settling your dispute, you have a difficult decision to make. Several questions you will want to consider in deciding whether to go ahead with a hearing are discussed below.

- *How vital is the issue?* You will want to weigh the impact of the issue on your child's current and future educational experience. Its importance will vary with the individual child. For example, speech therapy may be more essential for some children than for others.
- *How strong is my case?* Take stock by reviewing the appropriate laws and regulations, reviewing records that relate to the case, finding out about other cases that have been decided on similar issues, and consulting with parent organizations and an attorney.
- *How much resistance is the school district likely to offer?* The school district will go to greater lengths if officials believe that your position will involve the school system in considerable expense, or if the case might set a precedent that from their standpoint is undesirable, or if they fear a deluge of parent-initiated hearings. Expect strong resistance if you are seeking, for example, private-school placement at the school district's expense or a full-time aide for your mainstreamed child.
- *What will it cost?* You may incur considerable expense to retain representation by an attorney or advocate, hire expert witnesses, or get an independent educational evaluation. Some advocacy organizations or legal aid offices may provide free or low-cost representation, particularly if the issue has wide-ranging implications for other children with special needs. Congress has passed legislation (Public Law 99-372) that entitles parents who win legal cases relating to special education placement to collect attorneys' fees from schools.

- *Do I have the time?* A hearing typically lasts anywhere from a few hours to a few days. But you probably will spend considerably more time preparing for it.
- *Does my family have the emotional stamina?* The due-process hearing may prove emotionally draining and stressful for you, your child, and other family members. But you may also derive satisfaction and a sense of purpose from knowing that you are doing everything possible to give your youngster a sound educational program.
- *How will the hearing affect my relationship with the school?* By definition, a due-process hearing is an adversarial proceeding. It may strain your relationship with school officials. Loss of rapport may be of particular concern if your child's educational program requires a high degree of home-school cooperation.

Requesting a Hearing

If, having answered these questions for yourself, you want to proceed, your next step is to formally request a due-process hearing by sending a letter to the school superintendent or the director of special education or special services. (Don't request the hearing until you have done most of your preparation, since the hearing might be scheduled soon after the request.) Your letter should clearly identify you and your child, and state the reason for the request and the action sought. It should cite the relevant regulations. (Parent advocacy groups or an attorney can help you here.) Send the letter by certified mail, return receipt requested. Keep one copy for your files, and send another to the division of special education at the state department of education. A hearing officer appointed by the state usually takes responsibility for arranging the hearing and notifying the parties of the date and location.

Procedural Requirements

Federal and state regulations govern the nature and format of the due-process hearing. Since federal regulations provide minimal guidance on procedural matters, states have spelled out additional requirements. For this reason, be sure to consult both federal and state regulations when you prepare for the hearing. On the whole, these regulations aim to provide an uncomplicated system for resolving disputes fairly and quickly. Additional federal requirements, which must be followed in all states, are described below.

• The hearing must be conducted by the state department of education or by the school district responsible for educating your child.

• The school district must notify you of any free or low-cost legal and other relevant services available locally.

• The hearing officer must be impartial: he or she cannot be employed by the school district or have a personal or professional connection with the case that would compromise objectivity.

• The hearing officer's decision is final unless appealed. If the hearing is conducted by the school district, it can be appealed to the state department of education; if it is conducted by the state, it can be appealed to a state or federal civil court. If the state department of education turns down your appeal, you can bring your appeal one step further to state or federal court.

• The hearing officer must reach a decision and send it to you within forty-five days of the date that you first requested a hearing. When the state department of education reviews a case on appeal, it must reach a decision and send it to you within thirty days of the review request. Extensions may be granted.

• Your child remains in the present educational placement during the hearing unless you and the school district agree otherwise. For example, if the sole issue of a hearing is whether your child qualifies for psychological counseling as a related service, you and the school district can agree to implement all other aspects of the IEP, including the special education placement.

Your Rights

At the hearing, both you and the school district have the right to

• have access to all school records concerning your child;
• be represented by an attorney or advocate;
• present evidence, examine and cross-examine witnesses, and compel the attendance of witnesses, including school officials;
• prohibit the use at the hearing of any evidence not revealed to you at least five days before the hearing;
• have a taped or written record of the hearing; and
• receive the hearing officer's decision in writing.

In addition, you, but not the school district, have the right to

• open the hearing to the public; and
• have your child present.

Preparing for the Hearing

Once you decide to request a hearing, you must be ready to commit considerable time and effort to preparing your case, whether you have representation or not. Getting the program you want for your child may depend largely on how thorough and systematic you are in your preparation. The comprehensive file described in chapter 5 can help immeasurably in gathering evidence and identifying witnesses to substantiate your assertions. You and your representatives will want to consult applicable state and federal regulations as well as information on the hearing process. *So You're Going to a Hearing*, described at the end of this chapter, is especially useful.

A key ingredient in your preparation is finding knowledgeable representation. (This may or may not be a lawyer.) While you are entitled to represent yourself at the hearing (and some parents have done so competently and successfully), you may lack the grasp of hearing procedures, legislative regulations, and the principles of case organization that make for an effective presentation. Even if you have the know-how, you may profit from the calm detachment of a representative. Bear in mind that your school district probably has experience in the hearing process, and may well be represented by attorneys who will not hesitate to use a variety of legal tactics to advance the school's position. After all, that is what they are paid for.

When you shop for representation, look for an individual who knows the hearing process and is familiar with applicable state and federal regulations. A grasp of the principles and practices of special education is essential, and a commitment to the rights of students who have disabilities is important. Sound case-presentation skills are crucial.

How do you find this person? You might speak with your attorney, who probably has the skills to deal with the complex legal issues that occasionally arise at hearings. But your attorney may lack the knowledge of special education law or practices. If you don't think he or she has the experience and knowledge in this specialized area, ask for a referral to a lawyer who does. Or consider representation by a parent advocate who can be contacted through a local parent advocacy organization. These advocates often have the necessary combination of hearing experience, knowledge of regulations and procedures, and a grasp of special education practices. Talk with other parents and advocacy groups and interview prospective representatives before making this important decision.

The checklist presented in Figure 7.1 suggests steps that you and your representatives can follow when you negotiate a dispute with the school district and prepare your case for a due-process hearing.

FIGURE 7.1 Conflict-Resolution Checklist

This checklist is designed to help you and your representatives respond to conflicts in a systematic way and prepare effectively for due-process hearings. (It can also be used by school officials, although the items reflect the parent's perspective.)

YES   NO

☐ ☐ 1. Have you clearly identified the specific issue of disagreement and the change you are seeking?

☐ ☐ 2. Have you requested an independent educational evaluation, if appropriate?

☐ ☐ 3. Have you requested an IEP review, if appropriate?

☐ ☐ 4. Have you requested an early reevaluation of your child, if appropriate?

☐ ☐ 5. Have you met informally with school officials to try to resolve the dispute?

☐ ☐ 6. Have you requested mediation to resolve the dispute?

☐ ☐ 7. Have you considered registering a formal complaint with a state or federal agency if the school fails to comply with a law or regulation?

☐ ☐ 8. Have you determined whether the issue is appropriate for requesting a due-process hearing?

☐ ☐ 9. Have you familiarized yourself with federal and state regulations related to hearing procedures?

☐ ☐ 10. Have you determined the state and federal criteria that must be met to maintain your position?

☐ ☐ 11. Have you gathered information on the issues in the dispute by talking with advocacy organizations, specialists, and other parents and by reviewing appropriate literature?

☐ ☐ 12. Have you obtained from the school system and other sources copies of materials related to your child's education (evaluation reports, teachers' reports, work samples, the IEP, etc.) and reviewed them?

☐ ☐ 13. Have you observed your child in his or her present educational setting and observed and gathered information on any other educational settings relevant to the dispute?

☐ ☐ 14. Have you prepared a chronology of your child's involvement in the special education process?

☐ ☐ 15. Have you weighed the various considerations in deciding whether to request a due-process hearing?

☐ ☐ 16. Have you formally requested a hearing in a letter to the school?

☐ ☐ 17. Have you obtained an attorney or advocate experienced and knowledgeable in special education law and practices to represent you?

☐ ☐ 18. Have you used the information you have gathered to formulate your position and develop your hearing strategies?

☐ ☐ 19. Have you anticipated the school district's position and its supporting arguments?

☐ ☐ 20. Have you requested a pre-hearing conference to clarify hearing procedures and stipulate areas of agreement?

☐ ☐ 21. Have you determined which witnesses you wish to call to support your position?

☐ ☐ 22. Have you arranged for their appearance, including informing the school which staff members are requested, and have you sought subpoenas if necessary?

☐ ☐ 23. Have you selected and prepared documents, charts, and other exhibits you plan to introduce as evidence?

☐ ☐ 24. Have you provided to the school district, at least five days prior to the hearing, copies of all documents to be used as evidence and a list of witnesses you plan to call?

☐ ☐ 25. Have you obtained the same information from the school district at least five days before the hearing?

☐ ☐ 26. Have you prepared questions to ask your witnesses and those called by the school district?

☐ ☐ 27. Have you adequately prepared your witnesses by discussing the nature of the dispute, the materials they should bring, the questions you plan to ask, and the questions the school district may ask?

☐ ☐ 28. Have you decided whether to include your child in the hearing?

☐ ☐ 29. Have you decided whether the hearing is to be open or closed to the public?

☐ ☐ 30. Have you requested an interpreter, if necessary?

☐ ☐ 31. Have you written an opening statement?

☐ ☐ 32. Have you assessed and challenged, if necessary, the impartiality of the hearing officer?

☐ ☐ 33. Have you attended another due-process hearing to familiarize yourself with the format and procedures?

☐ ☐ 34. Have you rehearsed your presentation and role-played different situations?

The Hearing Process

The hearing officer often asks both parties to attend a brief conference before the hearing, where ground rules and procedures are explained, and areas of agreement and disagreement are clarified.

The hearing's format varies somewhat depending on the state and the individual who is presiding. Federal law does not require hearing officers to come from a particular profession, so they have diverse backgrounds and varying competencies. Many, but not all, are attorneys or educators. While the hearing is a legal proceeding, it is usually more flexible than a courtroom proceeding and the hearing officer has greater discretion than a judge in adapting the procedures.

Usually five to fifteen persons are present. The hearing, which typically is tape recorded, generally consists of these steps:

- *Official Opening.* The hearing officer makes a short statement identifying the persons in attendance, the reasons for the hearing, and the procedures to be followed.
- *Opening Statements.* You or your representative summarize your position, the supporting legal and factual arguments, and the action you are seeking. The school district does the same.
- *Case Presentations.* Each side presents evidence to support its claims, and witnesses give testimony. Each side may question their own witnesses as well as those called by the other side. The hearing officer may also ask questions of the witnesses. The rules of evidence are looser than in a courtroom proceeding; any form of evidence is usually admissible as long as it is relevant to the issue in dispute. This is your opportunity to make and support *all* of your points, since the hearing officer's decision will be based on the information offered during this stage.
- *Closing Statements.* You (and the school district) review the merits of your position, point to the weaknesses of the other side's position, and restate the action you seek.
- *Official Closing.* The hearing officer may explain the decision process and appeals procedures.

After the Hearing

After reviewing the evidence and testimony, the hearing officer must provide you (and the school district) with a written decision within forty-five days of the hearing request. State law may require a decision within a specific number of days after the hearing's conclusion. The written opinion should include, at a minimum, a summary of the issues and the evidence, findings of fact, conclusions, and a clear statement of the decision. The hearing officer can decide in favor of your position or the school district's position, or can issue another ruling (different from that requested by either party) based on the hearing officer's own judgment of your child's best educational interests. For example, the hearing officer can order a change in placement or new services for your child that must be provided by the district even if those services are not currently available; the IEP must be revised accordingly.

You and the school district both have the right to appeal this decision to the state department of education or to a state or federal civil court. States typically impose time limits on when the case can be appealed. The state department of education may request additional written evidence and conduct further hearings as part of its review.

The final decision is not really the last word on the matter. You and the school district now need to achieve a cooperative working relationship so that the letter and spirit of the decision can be carried out. Otherwise, new problems may crop up. For example, a school district may interpret the hearing officer's decision narrowly, meeting only its bare requirements; in some cases a district may not fully comply with the decision. Or, embittered by the outcome, you might fail to provide the ongoing support of the program on which your child's progress may hinge.

If you feel that the letter or spirit of the decision is not being carried out, you may have only limited and often ineffectual options, including trying to persuade or pressure the school district to modify its position, lodging a formal complaint with the state department of education, or requesting another hearing. Some states have, however, instituted formal procedures to monitor compliance with the decision.

Your relationship with the school may be strained and awkward after the hearing, but unless you decide to withdraw your child from the public school setting altogether, you will want to continue to work together. For this reason, it is critical that during every step of the conflict-resolution process, each side shows respect for the other's viewpoint; personal feelings are less important than the ongoing home-school alliance that can help your child to learn effectively.

FOR FURTHER INFORMATION

Bateman, B. (1980). *So you're going to a hearing: Preparing for a Public Law 94–142 due process hearing.* Northbrook, Ill.: Hubbard. This compact, information-filled guide describes practical strategies for preparing for and engaging in a hearing.

Budoff, M., Orenstein, A., and Kervick, C. (1982). *Due process in special education: On going to a hearing.* Cambridge, Mass.: Ware. Discusses the experiences of parents who went through the hearing process based on a wide-ranging study conducted in Massachusetts. Provides instructive insights into the problems of translating the noble purpose of the due-process hearing into an effective and efficient conflict-resolution procedure.

Gallant, C. B. (1982). *Mediation in special education disputes.* Silver Spring, Md.: National Association of Social Workers. While much of this book is geared toward educators, it also offers parents a useful overview of the mediation process.

Pullin, D. (1982). *Special education: A manual for advocates.* Cambridge, Mass.: Center for Law and Education. A two-volume publication that details special education practices, federal statutes and regulations, the hearing process, and applicable federal court decisions.

Shrybman, J. A., and Matsoukas, G. (1982). *Due process in special education.* Rockville, Md.: Aspen Systems. A very detailed account of the due-process safeguards available to special education students and their parents, the legal obligations of school districts, and procedures and strategies used in due-process hearings.

Appendix A:
Warning Signs that Suggest
a Possible Educational Disability

The following is a detailed (but not exhaustive) list of behaviors and characteristics that may suggest a possible educational disability. It can best be used *not* to detect an educational disability, but rather to decide whether your child might need further evaluation by a professional evaluation team. As you go through this list, you should keep certain principles in mind.

1. Many children who do not have educational disabilities show some of these characteristics. In most cases, there is little need for concern unless your youngster exhibits many of these characteristics or several clustered in one category, or unless your child shows one or more of these forms of behavior continuously and intensely.

2. Many of these characteristics are typical of very young children, and only suggest a possible disability if your son or daughter exhibits them after a certain age. For example, kindergarten and first-grade children often reverse letters when they write; there is more reason for concern, however, if your child still reverses letters in the third grade. Some of the characteristics in the list suggest an approximate age by which most children master a skill. Review these statements with caution: the fact that your youngster has not attained a skill by the expected age may mean a delay in development of that skill rather than an educational disability.

3. These characteristics may be present in some situations and not in others. It is not uncommon for a teacher to observe behavior of which you may not be aware, since the school setting often imposes different demands and elicits different responses than the home setting. You therefore might want to ask about your child's behavior in the classroom rather than assume that it mirrors what you see at home.

4. A particular form of behavior may be the direct expression of an educational disability (a primary problem) or it may be a "side effect" of another difficulty (a secondary problem). For example, your daughter's angry outbursts may stem from intense frustration at her reading difficulties. In other words, the behavior problem may be sec-

ondary to the learning problem. Differentiating between primary and secondary problems is a key to understanding your child's needs and planning helpful programs.

Health. Your child may have a health-related problem if he or she

> is lethargic and sluggish;
> tires easily, falls asleep during class;
> appears wan and pale;
> drools;
> requests to go to nurse often;
> complains often of headaches, stomachaches, nausea, or dizziness;
> appears malnourished.

*Hearing.** Your child may have a hearing problem if he or she

> consistently turns one side of head toward source of sound;
> holds hand behind ear when listening;
> turns television sound up loud;
> appears inattentive to what people are saying;
> often requests that questions or directions be repeated;
> is reluctant to participate in class discussion;
> provides irrelevant or inappropriate responses to questions;
> has speech articulation difficulties;
> speaks very loudly or very softly.

Vision. Your child may have a visual problem if he or she

> rubs eyes or squints frequently;
> complains often of dizziness or headaches;
> tilts head in unusual manner;
> is hesitant to participate in visually demanding games or tasks;
> holds books close to or far from eyes;
> has difficulty reading or copying from blackboard;
> confuses letters while reading (for example, *c* and *e*, or *g* and *q*);
> has difficulty aligning written work;
> chooses unusual color combinations.

---

*Adapted from a list provided by the U.S. Public Health Service, 5600 Fishers Lane, Rockville, MD 20857.

Visual Perception. Your child may have difficulty with visual perception if he or she

> has problems discriminating among different shapes and letters;
> has a hard time retaining visual images;
> reverses letters or numbers while reading or writing after age eight (for example, confuses *b* and *d* or *p* and *q*, reads *12* for *21*, writes *gril* for *girl*);
> reads words backwards (for example, reads *was* for *saw* or *on* for *no*);
> is easily distracted by extraneous visual images (for example, has difficulty with math problems grouped on a page but can do them when each is on a separate page);
> has spatial orientation difficulties (for example, is often confused in getting around school);
> does not consistently know left from right by age eight.

Receptive Language. Your child may have difficulty understanding language if he or she

> has difficulty discriminating between sounds (for example, between consonant blends or between similar-sounding words such as *put* and *pat*);
> often fails to understand oral or written information (for example, teacher directions);
> frequently confuses language concepts (for example, *on* and *in* or *before* and *after*);
> has difficulty retaining what is said in correct sequence (for example, cannot follow two-step directions correctly by age five);
> is unable to understand when background noise is present;
> repeats a request or question before responding;
> responds with an irrelevant answer.

Expressive Language. Your child may have difficulties with oral and written expression if he or she

> is delayed in reaching speech milestones (for example, does not say first word by age eighteen months or speak in complete sentences by age four);
> distorts sounds or mispronounces words (for example, says *aminal* for *animal* or *hopsital* for *hospital*);

> fails to pronounce the medial (middle) or final sounds of words;
> stutters or hesitates to significant degree while speaking;
> confuses verb tenses or uses pronouns inappropriately;
> begins or ends statements in the middle of a sentence;
> has difficulty recalling names of familiar objects or people;
> is unable to transfer thoughts to paper coherently (for example, writing is characterized by run-on sentences, incomplete sentences, or poor sequencing).

Thinking. Your child may have difficulty with orderly, rational thinking if he or she

> thinks in a disorganized and incoherent manner;
> has difficulty understanding abstract concepts (for example, interprets proverbs in concrete manner);
> is preoccupied with details and misses the "big picture";
> does not consistently relate actions to their consequences or understand cause-effect relationships;
> draws inappropriate conclusions;
> misperceives social situations or reactions of other people;
> has a problem in making decisions.

Learning. Your child may have a learning problem if he or she

> cannot identify letters of alphabet by age six;
> has poor retention of learned material such as math facts, spelling words, days of week, telling time ("she seems to know it one day but not the next");
> completes work much more slowly than others;
> has difficulty working independently and needs frequent teacher supervision;
> has a hard time organizing self and materials (for example, forgets to bring proper materials home or to class, misplaces homework or turns it in late consistently, has cluttered desk);
> has considerable difficulty in sounding out words;
> reads one year below grade level in early grades or two years below grade level in later grades;
> makes unusual spelling errors;
> achieves poorly in some academic areas and highly in others.

Fine-Motor Skills. Your child may be deficient in fine-motor skills if he or she

has difficulty manipulating small items;
is unable to unbutton by age four or tie shoelaces by age six;
has an awkward pencil grip;
cannot draw a circle by age three-and-a-half or four;
is unable to stay on the line while writing;
has too little or too much space between words;
forms letters poorly.

Gross-Motor Skills. Your child may be deficient in gross-motor skills if he or she

frequently stumbles or knocks into things;
has difficulty catching or throwing;
has poor balance (for example, is unable to balance on one foot
    for five seconds by age five);
is unable to walk a straight line or on tiptoe;
runs or jumps awkwardly;
cannot skip by age seven;
has not established either right- or left-handedness by age five.

Activity Level. Your child may have a below-normal or above-normal activity level if he or she

seems in almost constant motion;
is fidgety in seat;
is a restless sleeper;
lacks patience in waiting for turn (for example, calls out in class
    without raising hand);
frequently acts before thinking without concern for conse-
    quences;
hurries through schoolwork, giving rise to careless errors;
is much *less* active physically than peers (for example, moves in
    a slow and listless manner).

Attention Level. Your child may have an inadequate attention span if he or she

has difficulty concentrating for even brief periods;
is easily distracted by background noise;
often appears to daydream;
takes long time to complete task.

Social and Emotional Status. Your child may have social and emotional difficulties if he or she

> is readily frustrated and gives up easily;
> is prone to unpredictable and marked emotional changes ("he is happy one minute and in tears the next");
> shows signs of anxiety (for example, is fidgety, displays nervous habits, or complains often of physical ailments);
> appears sad more often than happy;
> displays low self-confidence (for example, is easily discouraged or makes self-disparaging comments);
> is overly dependent on adults;
> has difficulty accepting changes in routine;
> has trouble relating to peers or sustaining friendships;
> is withdrawn and shy;
> is defiant and hostile toward authority figures;
> is physically or verbally aggressive toward peers.

Appendix B:
Organizations
and Information Resources

This is a select list of national organizations that provide information, support, and advocacy services to people who have disabilities, their parents, and the professionals who work with them. Some of these organizations have local chapters for which addresses can usually be found in telephone directories. A more comprehensive listing of organizations as well as descriptions of the services they provide may be found in the *Directory of National Information Sources on Handicapping Conditions and Related Services*, published in 1982 by the Clearinghouse on the Handicapped of the U.S. Department of Education. It can be purchased from the Superintendent of Documents, U.S. Government Printing Office, Washington, DC 20402; ask for publication no. E—82–22007.

You can also seek help or information from state-based organizations (for example, the Ohio Coalition for the Education of Handicapped Children, the Maine Parent Federation, and the Parent Information Center of Delaware), many of which provide parent-training programs. Special education professionals within your local school district or at the state department of education can assist you in finding appropriate organizations within your state. The National Information Center for Handicapped Children and Youth, listed below, can also inform you of parent and advocacy groups in your local area.

Alexander Graham Bell Association for the Deaf
3417 Volta Place, N.W.
Washington, DC 20007
1-202-337-5220

American Association of the Deaf-Blind
1220 East-West Highway
Silver Spring, MD 20910
1-301-589-7279

American Association on Mental Deficiency
1719 Kalorama Road, N.W.
Washington, DC 20009
1-202-387-1968

American Camping Association
Bradford Woods
Martinsville, IN 46151
1-317-342-8456

American Coalition of Citizens with Disabilities
1012 14th Street, N.W.
Washington, DC 20005
1-202-628-3470

American Council of the Blind
1211 Connecticut Avenue, N.W.
Washington, DC 20006
1-202-833-1251; 1-800-424-8666

American Council on Rural Special Education
National Rural Development Institute
Western Washington University
359 Miller Hall
Bellingham, WA 98225
1-206-676-3576

American Occupational Therapy Association
1383 Piccard Drive
Rockville, MD 20850
1-301-948-9626

American Physical Therapy Association
1111 North Fairfax Street
Alexandria, VA 22314
1-703-684-2782

American Society for Deaf Children
814 Thayer Avenue
Silver Spring, MD 20910
1-301-585-5400

American Speech-Language-Hearing Association
10801 Rockville Pike
Rockville, MD 20852
1-301-897-5700

Association for Children and Adults with Learning Disabilities
4156 Library Road
Pittsburgh, PA 15234
1-412-341-1515; 1-412-341-8077

Association for Persons with Severe Handicaps
7010 Roosevelt Way, N.E.
Seattle, WA 98115
1-206-523-8446

Association for Retarded Citizens of the United States
2501 Avenue J
Arlington, TX 76011
1-817-640-0204

Association on Handicapped Student Service Programs in Post-
   Secondary Education
P.O. Box 21192
Columbus, OH 43221
1-614-488-4972

Boy Scouts of America
Scouting for the Handicapped Division
1325 Walnut Hill Lane
Irving, TX 75062
1-214-659-2127

Center for Independent Living
2539 Telegraph Avenue
Berkeley, CA 94704
1-415-841-4776

Center for Law and Education
Gutman Library
6 Appian Way
Cambridge, MA 02138
1-617-495-4666

Children's Defense Fund
122 C Street, N.W.
Washington, DC 20001
1-202-628-8787; 1-800-424-9602

Citizen's Alliance to Uphold Special Education
313 South Washington Square
Lansing, MI 48933
1-517-485-4084

Clearinghouse on the Handicapped
Office of Special Education and Rehabilitative Services
Department of Education
Switzer Building
Washington, DC 20202
1-202-732-1241

Closer Look/Parents' Campaign for Handicapped Children and
    Youth
1201 Sixteenth Street, N.W.
Washington, DC 20036
1-202-822-7900

Coordinating Council for Handicapped Children
220 South State Street, Room 412
Chicago, IL 60604
1-312-939-3513

Council for Exceptional Children
1920 Association Drive
Reston, VA 22091
1-703-620-3660

Developmental Disabilities Administration
U.S. Department of Health and Human Services
200 Independence Avenue, S.W.
Washington, DC 20201
1-202-245-2890

Disability Rights Center
1346 Connecticut Avenue, N.W.
Washington, DC 20036
1-202-223-3304

Education Law Center
155 Washington Street, Room 209
Newark, NJ 07102
1-201-624-1815

Federation for Children with Special Needs
312 Stuart Street, 2nd Floor
Boston, MA 02116
1-617-482-2915

The Foundation for Children with Learning Disabilities
99 Park Avenue
New York, NY 10016
1-212-687-7211

Girl Scouts of the U.S.A.
Scouting for Handicapped Girls Program
830 Third Avenue
New York, NY 10022
1-212-940-7500

Higher Education and the Handicapped
1 Dupont Circle, N.W.
Washington, DC 20036
1-800-54-HEATH

Joseph P. Kennedy, Jr. Foundation
1350 New York Avenue, N.W.
Suite 500
Washington, DC 20005
1-202-393-1250

National Association of Vocational Education
    Special Needs Personnel
c/o Dr. Sheila Feichtner
Reschini House
Indiana University of Pennsylvania
Indiana, PA 15705
1-412-357-4434

National Committee for Citizens in Education
410 Wilde Lake Village Green
Columbia, MD 21044
1-301-997-9300
1-800-638-9675

National Federation of the Blind
1800 Johnson Street
Baltimore, MD 21230
1-301-659-9314

National Handicapped Sports
    and Recreation Association
10085 West 18th Avenue
Lakewood, CO 80215
1-303-232-4575

National Information Center for Handicapped
    Children and Youth
1555 Wilson Boulevard, Suite 508
Rosslyn, VA 22209
1-703-522-3332

National Network of Learning Disabled Adults
P.O. Box Z
East Texas State University
Commerce, TX 75428

Office for Civil Rights
U.S. Department of Education
Room 5000 Switzer Building
330 C Street, S.W.
Washington, DC 20202
1-202-732-1213

Orton Dyslexia Society
724 York Road
Baltimore, MD 21204
1-301-296-0232; 1-800-222-3123

Parent Advocacy Coalition for Educational Rights
4826 Chicago Avenue
Minneapolis, MN 55417
1-612-827-2966

Parent Educational Advocacy Training Center
228 South Pitt Street, Room 300
Alexandria, VA 22314
1-703-836-2953

President's Committee on Employment of the Handicapped
1111 20th Street, N.W., 6th floor
Washington, DC 20036
1-202-653-5044

President's Committee on Mental Retardation
Room 4063 HHS North Building
Washington, DC 20201
1-202-245-7634

Recording for the Blind
20 Roszel Road
Princeton, NJ 08540
1-609-452-0606

Special Education Programs
U.S. Department of Education
Switzer Building
330 C Street, S.W.

Washington, DC 20202
1-202-732-1007

Special Olympics
1701 K Street, N.W., Suite 203
Washington, DC 20006
1-202-331-1346

Western Law Center for the Handicapped
1420 West 9th Street
Los Angeles, CA 90015
1-213-736-1031

Appendix C: Glossary

You may come across the following terms when you meet with school staff or review an evaluation report or an IEP. You may be familiar with the general meanings of some of these terms, but not necessarily with their specific educational meaning. In selecting terms for inclusion in this glossary, I have given priority to those describing programs, procedures, and regulations basic to special education. Space limitations preclude listing all terms that describe educational disabilities, characteristics of children with special needs, or specific teaching strategies and techniques. Those terms can be found in more comprehensive glossaries such as the *Special Education Dictionary*, ed. Edmond Gold (Westbury, NY: Heliodor Publications, 1983), or Lillie Pope's, *Learning Disabilities Glossary* (Brooklyn, NY: Book-Lab, 1976).

Accommodation. Modification of teaching approach or school program to meet the educational needs of a particular child.

Achievement test. A test that measures what a child has learned in a particular area.

Adaptive behavior. Skills needed by a child to function effectively and appropriately for his or her age in the school, family, and community settings.

Affective education. A formal program to help children understand and deal with their own and others' feelings, and to interact appropriately with others.

Anecdotal record. A written description of a child's behavior in a specific situation.

Annual goal. A statement contained in the IEP of what a child is expected to learn in a specific area in one year.

Annual review. A review of a child's special education program to be held at least once a year to assess progress and determine whether any program changes are necessary for the following year.

Appropriate. In the context of a "free appropriate public education," refers to an educational program that is capable of meeting the educational needs of a child who has an educational disability.

Aptitude test. A test that estimates a child's capacity for learning.

Assessment. See *Evaluation.*

Barrier-free. Refers to a public building that is free of obstacles that impede access to people who have physical disabilities.

Behavior modification. The systematic application of the principles of learning theory to change behavior by modifying events that precede or follow the behavior.

Buckley Amendment. The federal "right-to-know" law that entitles parents access to their children's school records, restricts the release of records to other people, and provides a mechanism through which parents may challenge information contained in the records. More formally called the Family Educational Rights and Privacy Act of 1974.

Career education. An educational program that aims to develop awareness and foster exploration of career alternatives as well as develop vocational and social skills appropriate to the world of work.

Child find. The continuous efforts of a school district to identify all children from birth to age twenty-one in its area who may have educational disabilities and need special education.

Chronological age (CA). The child's actual age, usually stated in years and months (for example, 11-2 means 11 years, 2 months).

Classification. The process of determining eligibility for special education and of assigning a formal term to describe a child's educational disability. Also called "labeling."

Confidentiality. The obligation of persons with knowledge about a child's educational history or characteristics to share that information only with others directly involved with that child and only when it is potentially helpful to him or her. Access to a child's written education records is governed by federal law (see *Buckley Amendment*).

Consent. Written parent approval required for the evaluation of their child or for initial placement of a child in a special education setting, according to Public Law 94–142.

Criterion-referenced test. A test that results in a profile of skills a child has learned and not learned, without comparison to the performance of other children.

Developmental delay or lag. A temporary delay in the child's development of a skill or characteristic. Also called a maturational lag.

Diagnostic test. A test that provides an in-depth assessment of a skill area, including strengths and weaknesses and error patterns.

Disability. See *Educational disability*.

Due process. A system of procedures designed to ensure that individuals are treated fairly and have an opportunity to contest decisions made about them. The due-process requirements of Public Law 94–142 and Section 504 are intended to safeguard the right of children who have disabilities to a free appropriate public education.

Due-process hearing. A formal hearing before an impartial hearing officer or panel to resolve a conflict between parents and the school district regarding the identification, evaluation, or educational placement of a child.

Early intervention. The provision of educational services at an early age for children with learning difficulties to avoid more severe learning problems in later years.

Educational disability. A specific cognitive, physical, or emotional problem that impedes the learning process to the extent that specially designed instruction is necessary for the person to learn effectively.

Evaluation. The process by which a team of professionals gathers information about a child's skills, deficits, aptitudes, interests, and personality variables from a variety of sources, including testing, observation, and other procedures, to guide decisions about the child's educational program. Often used interchangeably with "assessment."

Exceptional child. A child whose educational needs differ significantly from those of his or her same-age peers to the extent that specially designed instruction is warranted. Encompasses students who have special educational abilities (the gifted) and disabilities.

Fine-motor coordination. The ability to use the small muscles to accomplish tasks requiring precision such as writing, cutting, or sewing.

Formal test. A standardized evaluative measure, namely one that has explicit methods for administration and scoring and for which norms are available.

Frustration level. The level of an academic task at which a child begins to experience significant difficulty. The level of instruction should be below the frustration level.

Grade-level equivalent. A form for expressing a child's test performance. A child who performs on a test at the 3.3 grade level has achieved at a level typical of an "average" student in the third month (November) of the third grade.

Gross-motor coordination. The ability to use the large muscles in a coordinated, purposeful manner to engage in such activities as running, throwing, and kicking.

Handicapped child. The term used in federal and state law to designate a child who has a specific cognitive, physical, or emotional disability to the extent that specially designed instruction is necessary for him or her to learn effectively .

Handicapping condition. See *Educational disability.*

Hearing officer. An impartial individual who presides at a due-process hearing and is empowered to make a decision.

Homebound instruction. Temporary instruction at home, provided if a child is unable to attend school for medical reasons or if the school is in the process of arranging a special education placement.

Independent evaluation. Evaluation of a child by one or more professionals who have no formal relationship with the school district. Parents can request this evaluation if they disagree with the school's evaluation.

Independent level. The highest level of an academic task that a child can perform independently and relatively free of tension.

Independent living skills. Skills needed to care for oneself and to function effectively in a community setting (including, for example, personal hygiene, money management, cooking, use of public transportation, etc.).

Individualized education program (IEP). A written plan that a team composed of school staff, parents, and the child if appropriate, develops for every special education student. Must include, at a minimum, the child's current educational strengths and weaknesses, goals and objectives, educational services, start-up dates for those services, and procedures for program evaluation.

Individualized instruction. Academic instruction that is adapted to a particular child's individual needs and learning style.

Informal test. A nonstandardized evaluative measure usually designed by an individual (often a teacher) for a particular situation or purpose.

Instructional level. The level at which a child should be taught an academic task.

Instructional strategies. Specific teaching methods and materials to be used with a particular child.

Instrument. An educational term for a test or other measure used to evaluate a child, such as a behavior inventory filled out by a parent or a teacher.

Intelligence quotient (IQ). Score on an intelligence test for which 100 is the mean. Indicates a child's test performance relative to other children of the same age.

Intelligence test. A test used to measure overall capacity for learning. It provides a global estimate of scholastic aptitude, that is, a student's ability to succeed in school.

Itinerant teacher. A teacher who travels to different settings such as a regular classroom, hospital, or home to provide individualized instruction.

Learning style. The behaviors of a child that characterize his or her approach to learning.

Least restrictive environment. A standard established by Public Law 94–142 for special education placement. A child who has an educational disability must be allowed to participate in as much of the regular education program as is appropriate in view of his or her educational needs. The law holds that children with special needs must not be separated from students who do not have disabilities any more than is educationally necessary.

Local plan. A plan that each local school district must write on an annual basis describing its policies and procedures for meeting the educational needs of those children in the district who have disabilities and complying with state and federal laws.

Mainstreaming. The placement of a child who has an educational disability in an instructional setting in which most students do not have disabilities, in a manner that is educationally and socially beneficial to the child.

Mediation. A process for settling disputes between parents and school districts through the intervention of a neutral third party who tries to negotiate an agreement acceptable to both sides.

Mental age (MA). A form for expressing a child's performance on an intelligence test. A child who receives an MA of 8-4 has achieved a score comparable to an "average" child of 8 years, 4 months.

Minimum competency test. A test administered in many states to high school students that often determines eligibility for graduation. States differ in how they apply this requirement to special education students.

Multidisciplinary evaluation. A comprehensive evaluation of a child's educational status by a team of professionals from different disciplines and using a variety of sources of information. It is required by Public Law 94–142.

Multisensory approach. An instructional approach in which the teacher uses more than one of a child's senses to teach a task. Often used with children who have reading disabilities.

Nondiscriminatory evaluation. An evaluation in which the procedures and materials are not racially or culturally biased. Public Law 94–142 requires that an evaluation for special education placement be nondiscriminatory.

Norm. The average score on a test received by a group to which an individual's score can be compared.

Norm-referenced test. A test that yields a numerical score allowing comparison of a child's performance on that test with that of other children of the same age or grade who have taken it.

Occupational therapy. Treatment by an occupational therapist to improve an individual's ability to integrate different mental and motor processes in a purposeful and efficient manner.

On-the-job training. Provision of vocational training and experience at an actual job site (such as a retail store).

Percentile rank. A form for expressing a child's test performance relative to that of other children. A child who achieves a percentile rank of 54 has performed the same as or better than 54 percent of the children at that age or grade level who took the test.

Perceptual-motor tasks. Tasks that require the integration of perceptual and motor skills (for example, drawing a map).

Perceptual training. A program of exercises intended to correct weaknesses in perceptual or perceptual-motor skills. Its effectiveness in improving academic skills is unsubstantiated.

Physical therapy. Treatment by a physical therapist to improve an individual's motor skills and increase the strength and endurance of body parts.

Placement. The educational setting in which a student receives instruction (for example, a resource room).

Preacademic. A term that refers to basic skills (for example, the drawing of shapes) necessary to the acquisition of more formal academic skills.

Prehearing conference. A conference that usually precedes a due-process hearing at which the hearing officer clarifies ground rules and procedures and delineates areas of agreement and disagreement. In some states it may refer to a conference convened to try to resolve the parent-school dispute without going to a hearing.

Preliminary review. An initial review of the educational status of a youngster who is experiencing school-related difficulties, to determine whether a more in-depth evaluation is warranted.

Procedural safeguards. Legal regulations intended to safeguard the right of a child who has an educational disability to a free appropriate public education, and ensure that both child and parents receive the due process of law.

Projective test. A test usually administered by a psychologist to assess a child's emotional needs and concerns through his or her responses to unstructured, ambiguous questions or tasks.

Public Law 94–142. The primary federal legislative act involving the education of children who have educational disabilities. Called the Education for All Handicapped Children Act of 1975, this law aims to assure the availability of a "free appropriate public education" for every eligible child. It sets forth a range of school and parental responsibilities as well as procedural safeguards to ensure the due process of law.

Readiness. A level of skill development necessary to the learning of formal academic skills. A child at the reading readiness level is able, for example, to distinguish among the shapes of letters and retain their visual images.

Reevaluation. An evaluation of a student already receiving special education services to assess continuing eligibility and appropriateness of program. Must be conducted at least once every three years under federal law.

Referral. A formal request for evaluation for a child experiencing learning or behavior problems to determine eligibility for special education.

Related services. Support services needed by a child to benefit from special education (such as speech therapy or special transportation).

Reliability (of a test). The degree to which a test elicits consistent results over time and under various conditions.

Remediation. The process of correcting or strengthening areas of academic weakness.

Residential placement. A placement, usually arranged and paid for by a state agency or by the parents, where a child with special needs resides and typically receives academic instruction.

Resource room. A special education placement in which children receive intensive individual or small-group instruction for less than half the day. The children are usually instructed for the remainder of the day in a regular classroom.

Rules and regulations. Legal requirements written by executive agencies of the government that describe how a legislative act is to be carried out. Federal rules and regulations are issued in the *Federal Register.*

Screening. A program for identifying children in the general population who show signs of school-related problems and may therefore require a more in-depth evaluation to assess their eligibility for special education.

Section 504. A federal civil rights law passed in 1973 to eliminate discrimination against people with disabilities in federally funded programs. Requires that children with disabilities receive educational services and opportunities equal to those provided to other children.

Self-concept. The composite of perceptions an individual has about himself or herself.

Self-help skills. Skills related to the care of oneself such as eating, dressing, and grooming.

Sensory modalities. Specific channels through which a person receives information about the environment, including sight, sound, touch, taste, and smell.

Sheltered workshop. A structured employment program for individuals who have disabilities that prevent them from finding employment in the labor market.

Short-term instructional objective. Precise statement, described in terms of overt behavior, of what a child is expected to accomplish over a short period in a specific educational area. An intermediate step between the student's current skill level and the annual goal.

Social-skills training. Instruction and activities designed to develop skills needed to interact appropriately with others.

Special education. Specialized instruction for children who have educational disabilities based on a comprehensive evaluation. The instruction may occur in a variety of settings, but must be precisely matched to their educational needs and adapted to their learning style.

Special education class. An instructional setting for a relatively small group of students with similar special education needs. They typically attend the class for most of the school day. Often called a "self-contained class."

Speech and language therapy. An individualized program of instruction and exercises provided by a speech therapist and designed to correct or improve speech disorders or problems of language usage.

Standard deviation. A statistical concept that indicates the degree to which an individual's test score varies from the average score of a group.

Standardized test. A test that has explicit procedures for administration and scoring as well as norms or average scores for comparison purposes.

Standard score. A score that allows comparison with other students of the same age or grade level.

State plan. A plan that, by law, each state must write on an annual basis to describe its policies and procedures for complying with federal special education law.

Structure. An educational approach in which the teacher provides explicit and specific direction regarding the rules and routines of the classroom.

Surrogate parent. A knowledgeable individual assigned to represent the educational interests of a child in the absence of the parents.

Validity (of a test). The degree to which a test actually measures what it purports to measure.

Visual-motor integration. The ability to perceive visual images and reproduce them with a motor response (for example, copying from the blackboard).

Vocational education. An educational program that offers training in the technical skills of specific vocations and the competencies required to obtain and maintain a job.

Vocational rehabilitation. A program designed to assist people who have disabilities in obtaining employment by analyzing their vocational strengths and weaknesses, providing training if needed, and matching their vocational profile with appropriate types of employment.

Work experience. A component of a vocational education program in which an individual receives job training by working at an actual job site or in a simulated work setting.

Index

Index

Special education process *(ctd.)*
 IEP review, 94–95
 monitoring of progress, 89–90
 referral, 19–22, 98
 research findings, xiv, 9
Special education process, 15,
  16–17 *(Fig. 1.1)*
 eligibility determination and
  classification, 22–23, 25,
  34, 159
 evaluation, 6, 10, 22, 28–61
 flow chart, 15–17
 identification, 18–19, 20
 IEP development, 24, 71–95,
  106–10, 139–40
 IEP implementation, 24, 64,
  92, 111
 IEP review, 24, 66, 77, 93–95,
  98, 153
 reevaluation, 24–25, 40, 98,
  153
 referral, 19–22, 29, 30, 159
Special education regulations,
  state, xv, 4, 12, 22, 23, 26,
  35, 55, 78–79, 107, 161
Special education, salient
  features of, 10
Special education students. *See*
  Educational disability
Special education teachers, 10,
  78, 79, 104
Specialized materials and
  equipment, 10, 14, 78, 86,
  93, 94, 114
Special Olympics, 2
Speech, 42
Speech and language
  assessment, 56–57. *See also*
  Evaluation
Speech impairment, 39, 42
Speech synthesizer, 129
Speech therapy, 11, 57, 90, 159.
  See also Related services

Spina bifida, 58, 84
Standard deviation, 47
Standardization sample, 37, 47
Standardized test, 37. *See also*
  Tests
Stanine, 38
State commissioner of education,
  104
State department of education,
  4–5, 6, 104, 162
Step-parent, 10, 48
Stuttering, 12
Superintendent, 40, 104, 156, 161
Supplemental services, 78–79
Surrogate parent, 7–8
Suspension, 148–49

Task-oriented academic
  remediation, 53, 126–27
Teacher aide, 86
Terminology, special education,
  15, 182–191 *(App. C)*
Testing. *See* Evaluation; Tests
Test results
 grade-level equivalent, 38
 intelligence quotient, 38
 mental age, 38
 percentile, 38
 profile of skills, 38
 stanine, 38
Tests, 37–39. *See also*
  Evaluation.
 achievement, 37, 52
 aptitude, 37
 criterion-referenced, 37
 diagnostic, 37
 intelligence, 13, 37, 40, 41–48
 norm-referenced, 37
 standardized, 37
The Futures of Children, 23
Transportation, special, 85, 87,
  90–91. *See also* Related
  services